"That was excellently observed, say I, when I read a passage in an author, where his opinion agrees with mine. When we differ, there I pronounce him to be mistaken."

—*Jonathan Swift,* 1667–1745

Dean of St Patrick's Cathedral, Dublin

That's Ireland

An Irish Miscellany

Michael Nugent
Damian Corless

BLACKWATER PRESS

MICHAEL NUGENT

Michael Nugent is a writer and social campaigner. Previous books include the No 1 best-selling *Dear John: The John Mackay Letters* with Sam Smyth, *Dear Me* with Sam Smyth and Arthur Mathews, and *Ireland on the Internet: The Definitive Guide*. His next book is a study of happiness.

In *Dear John*, real-life Taoiseach Albert Reynolds helps fictitious 'John' to seek an IDA grant to produce dog bowls modelled as dinner plates, CJ Haughey wants to meet to discuss John's offer to fund a Bring Back CJ campaign, and Pope John Paul II prays for John's children who put condoms on the family chess set Bishops.

Contact: *michael@happying.com*

DAMIAN CORLESS

Damian Corless writes for a living. Previous books include *Loose Talk: The GUBU File,* the Aslan biography *Crazy World*, and *Pulp Friction: Irish Feuds & Public Ructions*. A former editor of *In Dublin, Magill* and *Ligger*, he has written television comedy for RTE and the BBC.

Pulp Friction chapters include The Screws Were All Astounded (Official Ireland v The Helicopter Song), There's A Big Fellow Called Salvador (Fr Michael Cleary v Religious Orthodoxy) and Shrubs Were Also Pulled Up (Peter Robinson v Poor Border Security). Signed, limited, numbered editions are available at €13 incl p&p.

Details: *damianc@tinet.ie*

Interior Design: Michael Nugent

Cover Design: Gerard Nugent

Published in Ireland by Blackwater Press,
Broomhill Business Park, Tallaght, Dublin 24

ISBN 1–84131–633–4

DEDICATIONS

From Michael to Anne, Michael, Mary, Paul, Louise, Gerard, José, the global fellowship of Nugents, Cotters & Hollidays, Carolyn, Arthur, Dan, Paul, Dave, Henry, René, Raisa, Earl Grey, Duck, Abu, all at Oscail and all who tolerated a year of hearing increasingly frequent updates about facts and lists.

From Damian to Martin, Kathleen, Mary, Ivan, Anne Marie, Ash, Toon, Helen and Sophie MacConkey for the miracle of family life; to Arthur Mathews, Ian O'Doherty, Sharon Dulux and the countless others who helped make this book one of the several wonders of the modern world.

To the fact that producing this book has reunited our fathers, Michael Nugent and Martin Corless, who studied together in the early days of recorded history.

To all at Blackwater Press, particularly John O'Connor, Margaret Burns, Melanie Gradtke and Gary Dermody.

To the Dewey Decimal System and the Internet.

To Bobby Ryan of Bohemians for scoring the goal against Shelbourne that won the league in 2003 (not directly relevant to the book, but always worth reminding people).

Website *www.thatsireland.net*
Email *info@thatsireland.net*

IT'S ONLY WORDS

In this book, unless the context requires otherwise...

THE WORD 'IRELAND' (POST-1922) MEANS

The 26 southern counties illegally run by treasonous Free State forces	The modern *29-county, 5-city Republic that is part of the EU	An alien Papist State interfering in internal UK affairs

THE WORDS 'NORTHERN IRELAND' MEAN

The six north-eastern counties still occupied by perfidious Albion	The Irish part of the UK, governed under the Good Friday Agreement	An integral part of the UK that is 'as British as Finchley'

* Ireland now has 29 counties, listed in the Local Govt Act 2001 (See p 15 of this book).

Feel free to translate any words in this book to reflect your personal political persuasions.

IT'S ONLY NAMES

ELECTION OF TDS BY FIRST LETTER OF SURNAME, 1922-2003

The case for Dáil candidates changing surnames to benefit from 'alphabetical voting'.

One in three of all TDs' names ever have started with A to D, and *four in ten* with A to F.

Over half have started with A to H, compared to *less than one in twenty* with S to Z.

Nearly one in four have started with M or O, reflecting 'Mac' and 'O' Irish surnames.

Each TD is counted only once, so re-election does not distort these figures.

Based on a study of 1,116 TDs elected 1922-2003. More details on pages 35 and 100.

BERTIE AHERN — 50-50 VISIONARY

"With hindsight, we all have 50-50 vision."

"We shouldn't upset the apple tart."

"There's one thing I can't do. I can't change the past. All that we're trying to do is clean up the past."

"We're not gonna hang anyone on the guillotine."

"Let's put the dirty linen — the *clean* linen — on the table."

"The cynics may point to the past but we live in the future."

"We haven't been able to do all that we can."

"The grass roots, or the rank and file, are now made from fibre optics."

"At present, I have my hand in a whole lot of dykes, trying to keep them in and keep people together."

"I could certainly drink a fair few pints of Bass and be capable of driving."

EARTHY IRISH PLACENAMES

Placename	*From Gaelic*	*Meaning*
Ballyhack	Baile Chac	Town of excrement
Ballyhackamore	Baile Hacamar	Town of the dungstand
Letterbreen	Leitir Bhruin	Hillside of the breast
Mace/Maas	Más	The buttock
Mausrower	Más Ramhar	The fat buttock
Tanderagee	Tóin Re Gaoith	Backside to the wind
Tearacht Island	Oileán Tiaracht	Buttock island
The Paps	An Dá Chích	The two breasts
Ton/Tonduff	Tóin/Tóin Dubh	Bottom/Black Bottom
Tonragee	Tóin Re Gaoith	Backside to the wind

1 Wexford; 2 Down; 3 Fermanagh; 4 Donegal, Galway, Mayo; 5, 7, 8 Kerry; 6 Armagh; 9 Monaghan; Donegal; 10 Mayo. Placenames like breast and buttock typically refer to the shape of hills.

THE THREE TYPES OF MUSIC PERFORMED AT GLENAMADDY'S 'SOUND OF MUSIC' CLUB

AS CATEGORISED BY THE MANAGEMENT

1. Country & Western 2. Pop 3. Mad Pop

IRISH POLITICAL ANAGRAMS

DAIL EIREANN	IDLE IN ARENA
FIANNA FAIL PD COALITION	*AN OLD PANIC AFFILIATION*
GREEN PARTY	ENERGY TRAP
THE FLOOD TRIBUNAL	*FLUENT BOLD HOT AIR*

EVOLUTION OF SCORING IN GAA

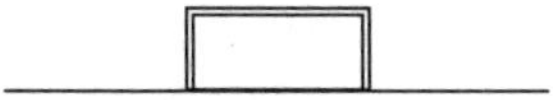

1884

Rectangular goal. 15 ft x 8 ft for football, 20 ft x 10 ft for hurling. No points. Whoever scores most goals wins.

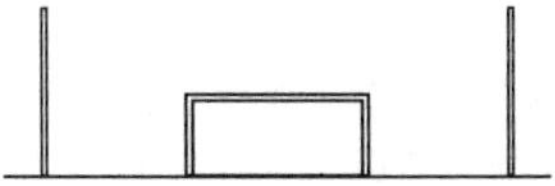

1886

Goal space 21 x 8 football, 21 x 10.5 hurling. Points space 21 ft either side. Points only count if goals are equal.

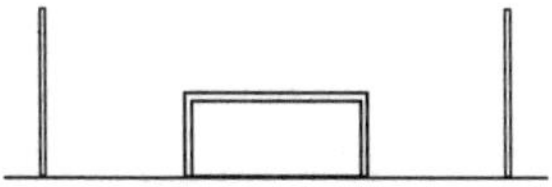

1895-6

Whoever scores the most points wins. In 1895, 1 goal = 5 points. From 1896, 1 goal = 3 points.

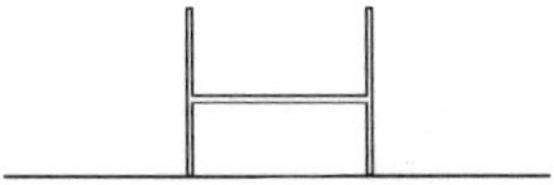

1910

Goal space is now 21 x 8 for football and hurling. Point zone is reduced to the ball going over the bar.

MEMBERS OF THE ROMAN CATHOLIC CHURCH

IRISH ECCLESIASTICAL RECORD, 1959

- Members In Some Way
  - In Act
    - Perfectly
      1. By Glory
      2. Souls In Purgatory (both outside jurisdiction of Roman Hierarchy)
      3. By Charity + Baptism + Submission to Roman Catholic Church ↑
    - Imperfectly
      - By Charity
        - Actual Baptism
          - Material Heretics ↑ and Schismatics ↑
          - Repentant Excommunicants
        - Baptism Voto
          - Catechumens
          - Material Pagans ↑
      - By Unformed Faith (Sinners)
        - Actual Baptism
          - Recognised ↓
          - Separated
            - Material Heretics ↓ and Schismatics ↓
            - All Formal Schismatics
            - Unrepentant Excommunicants
        - Not Baptised
          - Material Pagans ↓
      - By Sacramental Character w/o Grace
        - Recognised RCs
          - ↓ Secret Heretics
        - Separated
          - Apostates
          - Formal Heretics
  - In Potency
    - Unbaptised Sinners
      - Infants, Formal Sinners
- Not Members
  - The Damned (If baptised, character remains)
  - Children Dead w/o baptism (Probably)

↑ = State Of Grace ↓ = State Of Sin

THE SAFE CROSS CODE

WITH JUDGE FROM WANDERLY WAGON

Remember...
One! Look for a safe place.
Two! Don't hurry, stop and wait.
Three! Look all around and listen before you cross the road.

Remember...
Four! Let all the traffic past you.
Five! Then walking straight across, you
Six! Keep watching, that's the Safe Cross Code.

Know — The — Safe — Cross — Code.
Know the Code!

CONSUMER PRICE-WATCH

SINN FÉIN, DUP & ORANGE ORDER SHOPS

Shop	*Item*	*€*	*£*
SF	Playable Bodhrán with Party Logo	90.00	63.05
OO	Edinburgh Crystal Vase with Orange Logo	78.49	55.00
SF	Turf Model of the Easter Proclamation	44.44	31.13
SF	'Best of The Wolfe Tones Live' DVD	36.00	25.22
OO	King William or Queen Elizabeth Jewel	25.67	18.00
DUP	Party Cuff Link & Tie Pin Set	21.41	15.00
SF	Party T-Shirt or Polyester Irish Tricolour	15.00	10.51
DUP	Party Tie or 30th Anniversary Coin	14.27	10.00
OO	'Endangered Species' Ulster Scots Music CD	14.27	10.00
DUP	Queen Mother Memorial Plate	14.27	10.00
SF	Party Baseball Cap or Beanie Hat	13.97	9.79
DUP	Ulster Flag or 'Best of Ulster' Songbook	7.14	5.00
OO	King William Fine Bone China Thimble	2.35	1.65
SF	'Tiocfaidh Ár Lá' Glasgow Celtic Fanzine	1.90	1.49
OO	Flexible Bowler-Hatted-Man Fridge Magnet	1.43	1.00

Exchange rate 12 July 2003. Lapel badges are €5.08 SF; €3.57 DUP; €1.90 OO. Many SF items also available as IRA items, from same shop and at same price, but with no connection between them. Bat not included with SF baseball cap.

FIRST NIGHT OF TELIFÍS ÉIREANN, 1961

Inauguration by President De Valera, Taoiseach Lemass and Min for Posts & Telegraphs.	*Entertainment* by Maureen Potter, Jimmy O'Dea and Mary O'Hara.
Benediction of the Most Blessed Sacrament by Catholic Archbishop McQuaid.	*Review of 1961,* followed by greeting of the New Year from Dublin's O'Connell St.
Pearse & Yeats poems read by Siobhan McKenna and Michael MacLiammóir.	*New Year address* by the Catholic Primate of All-Ireland, Cardinal Dalton.

31 Dec 1961. In his inaugural address, President De Valera promoted the new medium by warning that, 'like atomic energy', TV can 'do irreparable harm' and 'can lead through demoralisation to decadence and disillusion'.

EXCLUSIVELY PEACEFUL MEANS

DECLARATION BY IRISH & BRITISH GOVERNMENTS

"We reaffirm our total and absolute commitment to exclusively democratic and peaceful means of resolving differences on political issues, and our opposition to any use or threat of force by others for any political purpose, whether in regard to this agreement or otherwise." — Good Friday Agreement, 1998

EXTRACTS FROM IRISH & BRITISH NATIONAL ANTHEMS

"We're children of a fighting race, that never yet has known disgrace, and as we march the foe to face, we'll sing a soldier's song."

"Our camp fires now are burning low. See in the east a silvery glow. Out yonder waits the Saxon foe, so sing a soldier's song."

"O Lord our God arise, scatter her enemies, and make them fall. Confound their politics, frustrate their knavish tricks, on Thee our hopes we fix, God save us all."

"Lord grant that Marshal Wade may by thy mighty aid victory bring. May he sedition hush, and like a torrent rush, rebellious Scots to crush, God save the King."

KERRY'S '4-IN-A-ROW' WINNERS, 1978-81

Charlie Nelligan 4

Jimmy Deenihan 4	John O'Keeffe 3 Vincent O'Connor 1	Mick Spillane 2 *Paudie Lynch 4*
Páidí Ó Sé 4	*Tim Kennelly 4*	Ger O'Keeffe 1 Mick Spillane 1

Jack O'Shea 4 *Seán Walsh 4*

Ger Power 3 Tommy Doyle 1	*Ogie Moran 4*	Pat Spillane 3 Tommy Doyle 1
Mikey Sheehy 4	Eoin Liston 3 Tommy Doyle 1	*John Egan 4*

All-Ireland football finals. Manager, Mick O'Dwyer. Beat Dublin (twice), Roscommon and Offaly by a combined score of 10-45 to 2-31. Subs used: Vincent O'Connor, Ger O'Driscoll, Ger O'Keeffe, Páidí O'Mahony and Pat Spillane. *Italics = started all four games.*

DON'T GO THERE

Placename	*From Gaelic*	*Meaning*
Ardnacrohy	Árd na Croiche	Height of the gallows
Ardnaree	Árd na Ria	Height of the executions
Cornafulla	Corr na Fola	Hill of the blood
Dromahair	Drom Dhá Eithiar	Ridge of two demons
Drumnafinnagle	Droim Na Fionghal	Ridge of the fratricide
Killare	Cill Air	Church of slaughter
Knockanarrigan	Cnoc an Aragain	Hill of the conflicts
Nart/Ardfert	An Fheart/Ard Fhearta	(Height of) the grave
Rath Loirc	Ráth Loirc	Fort of the murder
Aughnagomaun	Achadh na gComán	The hurling field

1 Limerick; 2 Mayo; 3 Roscommon; 4 Limerick; 5 Donegal (Fratricide = killing of brothers. Drumnafinnila, Limerick, also has the same meaning.); 6 Westmeath; 7 Wicklow; 8 Monaghan, Kerry; 9 Cork; 10 Tyrone.

THE FIRST WRITTEN RULES OF HURLING

In 1869 Galway's Killimor club adopted the first written rules of hurling. The first three were:

1. Each team, when hurling, must wear a different colour.

2. Three umpires to be appointed on each side who have power to order any hurler to cease playing, who in their opinion is under the influence of strong drink, who loses his temper or strikes an opponent intentionally. Should the hurler refuse to do so, the opposing team may claim the prize that is being played for.

3. Should any hurler, when jostling, use his hurl so as to bring it into contact with his opponent, with a view to injuring him, he must cease hurling when told to do so by any of the umpires. Penalty same as rule 2.

THE POETRY OF GEORGE HAMILTON

"Real Madrid are like a rabbit in the glare of the headlights in the face of Manchester United's attacks. But this rabbit comes with a suit of armour in the shape of two precious away goals."

"He caught that with the outside of his instep."

"The orange tide is lapping against the green door which refuses to open."

"The midfield are like a chef... trying to prise open a stubborn oyster to get at the fleshy meat inside."

"And there's no telling what the score will be if this one goes in."

"The Baggio brothers, of course, are not related."

"When I said they'd scored two goals, of course I meant they'd scored one."

GOODBYE TO OLD J ARTHUR

The theme song to RTE's comedy show 'Upwardly Mobile' originally went "so it's goodbye to old J Arthur, and it's hello to fine Chablis...". It was changed when RTE discovered that J Arthur refers not to Arthur Guinness, but to movie mogul J Arthur Rank. It is also rhyming slang for masturbation.

THE 29 COUNTIES OF IRELAND

Counties are changeable local administrative areas. Ireland's traditional 32 counties were gradually imposed after a 1569 Act gave "Her Majesty's laws free course throughout this whole realm of Ireland". Modern Irish and British Govts have changed them. Tipperary, once two ridings, is now two counties; Dublin was replaced by three counties and a city; and the six NI counties by 26 council districts.

CURRENT 29 COUNTIES & 5 CITIES OF IRELAND (LOCAL GOVT ACT 2001 SCH 5)

Counties: Carlow, Cavan, Clare, Cork, Donegal, Dun Laoghaire-Rathdown, Fingal, Galway, Kerry, Kildare, Kilkenny, Laois, Leitrim, Limerick, Longford, Louth, Mayo, Meath, Monaghan, Nth Tipperary, Offaly, Roscommon, Sligo, Sth Dublin, Sth Tipperary, Waterford, Westmeath, Wexford, Wicklow.

Cities: Cork, Dublin, Galway, Limerick, Waterford.

CURRENT 26 DISTRICTS & TRADITIONAL 6 COUNTIES OF NORTHERN IRELAND

Districts: Antrim, Ards, Armagh, Ballymena, Ballymoney, Banbridge, Belfast, Carrickfergus, Castlereagh, Coleraine, Cookstown, Craigavon, Derry, Down, Dungannon, Fermanagh, Larne, Limavady, Lisburn, Magherafelt, Moyle, Newry & Mourne, Newtownabbey, Nth Down, Omagh, Strabane.

Counties: Antrim, Armagh, Down, Fermanagh, Tyrone Derry or Londonderry.

THEOLOGICAL IMPLICATIONS OF "SHADY PRACTICES IN RACING & BETTING"

In 1893, the Catholic Church said it was morally "invalid" to bet on a race if you know the outcome. A horse owner "was not bound towards the betting man to run a *bona fide* race". However, if the owner bet on a later race, with the benefit of odds gained from a previous 'pulling', that bet was invalid.

By 1966 it was less rigid. "In the current climate, the betting and racing public accept as part and parcel of the sport a degree of interference with form and odds." If an owner conceals the form of his horse, "bookies may well be surprised by a well-planned coup, but this is part of the betting gamble".

Summarised from *Irish Ecclesiastical Review*, 1893 & 1966.

GRAHAM NORTON'S TOP 3 WEBSITES

findadeath.com *losers.org* *findagrave.com*

EUROVISION VOTE-RIGGING ALLEGATIONS

1968. 'Congratulations', written by Derryman Phil Coulter and sung by Cliff Richard for the UK, is the hot favourite, but 'tactical' (i.e. anti-British) voting relegates it to second place.

1970. Officials with the UK jury try to steer the jury's vote in favour of the Yugoslav entry and away from Ireland's 'All Kinds Of Everything', sung by Dana. Ireland win.

1971. As Ireland first hosts the contest (despite protests from Irish Cycling Association), a UK jury member reports that she has been offered a bribe in a Dublin pub.

2003. Russian 'lesbian' school-girl duo Tatu complain that they would have won if RTE had used its planned phone vote (the phone system had failed) instead of a jury vote.

FORMIDABLE IRISH WOMEN

Grace O'Malley, also called Grainneuaile. Lived in 1500s. Was a pirate, noblewoman, gambler, chieftain, mercenary. Her three galleys and 200 fighting men were based on Clare Island in Clew Bay.	*Máire Rua McMahon.* Lived in 1600s. Saved family castle by marrying Cromwellian soldier. Later charged with murdering her husband, and acquitted. By legend, her ghost is imprisoned in a hollow tree in Clarecastle.

IRISH-BASED NAZI PARTY MEMBERS

Colonel Fritz Brase	Director, Irish Army Music School
Dr Friedrich Herkner	Prof of Sculpture, College of Art
Dr Adolf Mahr	Director of the National Museum
Otto Reinhard	Director of Forestry, Dept of Lands
Friedrich Weckler	Chief Accountant with the ESB

In 1946, on his release from an internment camp, Dr Mahr applied to have his old job back as National Museum Director, but was turned down.

IRISH LAWS NOT REPEALED UNTIL 1983

Inheritance of Bastard	1238
Prohibition of Sale of Falcons, Hawks etc	1389
Part of Poynings' Act Annulling other Irish Laws	1495
The Act of Union	1800
Parts of Chimney Sweepers & Chimneys Act	1840
Dublin & Other Roads Turnpikes Abolition Act	1855
Poor Removal Act	1863
Lunacy (Vacating of Seats) Act	1886
Trading with the Enemy Act	1914
Output of Beer (Restriction) Act	1916

Statute Law Revision Act 1983.

EIGHT OIREACHTAS OBJECTIONS TO THE ADOPTION OF SUMMER TIME, 1923

1. It would be bad law because farmers ignore official time "except when they have to catch a train".

2. "I regret that an Irish government should follow in the footsteps of an English government."

3. The change would be "just to please a few lazy fellows in the towns who will not get up early. It is not necessary to put back the clock to make a man get up early; all he has to do is to shake himself. Why should the poor country people be caused all these annoyances to please the fellows in the towns?"

4. "It should be called the Lazy Man's Delusion Bill."

5. "In some parts of Kerry they are 42 minutes later than Greenwich, and when you add an hour to that you will have noon arriving about 10.15 in the morning."

6. The clocks should go back 35 minutes, not one hour.

7. No, not 35 minutes, they should go back 24 minutes.

8. "No self-respecting cow can expect to be milked at 2.30 am. According to this new Summer Time, in the West of Ireland cattle that in the ordinary course would be milked at 4.30 would now be milked at 2.30. The milk supply of the country is a very important matter."

1. W Cole TD; 2. & 3. Sen Moore; 4. & 5. Sen McLoughlin; 6. C Byrne TD; 7. J MacBride TD; 8. W Cole TD.

DEGREES OF INTOXICATION

Bollixed	Gee-eyed	Ossified	Rat-arsed
Buckled	Langered	Paralytic	Scuttered
* Circling over Shannon	Locked	Pissed	Sloshed
	Maggoty	Plastered	Stocious
Elephants	Mouldy	Polluted	Twisted

* In memory of Boris Yeltsin's visit to Shannon Airport, Oct 1994

CJ HAUGHEY — IN HIS OWN WORDS

TALKING TO *HOT PRESS* MAGAZINE, 1984

"I don't think I could say that I approve of youngsters knocking-off BMWs and so on. Although, I must admit, I always had a hidden desire to do something like that."

"I could instance a load of fuckers whose throats I'd cut and push over a cliff, but there's no percentage in that."

"I couldn't be anywhere (but) Dublin for Christmas, meeting all my friends, having a drink with them, giving out presents, getting presents. I'm a sucker for Christmas."

"Deep down I'm a very shallow person."

INSIGNIA ON BADGES OF KNIGHTS OF SAINT COLUMBANUS

Grand Knight	Cross with Sword	*Advocate*	Cross with Book
Deputy GK	Cross with Sword	*Warden*	Cross with Baton
Chancellor	Cross with Skull	*Registrar*	Cross with Scroll
Secretary	Cross with Feather	*Others*	Plain Cross

TWO OIREACHTAS ARGUMENTS FOR THE ADOPTION OF SUMMER TIME, 1923

1. Having a different time zone to NI would harden partition.

2. "You are continually meeting people in the country who, if it was 9 o'clock, were scratching their heads and wondering whether it was 8 or 10. They had great difficulties in making that calculation because of the mental strain it imposed, and were against the Summer Time for this reason apart from the political objection. If they had to think along mathematical lines it would perhaps be good for them."

1. Sen Douglas; 2. Sen Blythe.

FOUND IN GOODMAN-OWNED MEAT PLANTS, 1983-91

Bogus rubber stamps bearing mark of South African Customs.

Bogus invoices from phantom hauliers etc to value of millions.

Falsified papers claiming EC refunds for ineligible cheap meat.

Attempted fraud cover-up as staff 'assist' Customs inspection.

Offal, including hearts turned green, packed as Russian food aid.

"We don't like the word 'power'.
That is a sort of Leninist idea."
— Larry Goodman

IRISH FOOTBALL ANAGRAMS

LIAM BRADY	ADMIRABLY
DAVID O'LEARY	*LOVED A DIARY*
FOOTBALL ASSOCIATION OF IRELAND	TOTAL OFFICIAL LOONINESS ABROAD

NEATEST IRISH POPULATIONS

District	*Area*	*Population*
Kilbeggan	Mullingar Rural Area	1,000
Poleberry	Waterford City	1,000
Paulstown	Kilkenny Rural Area	500
Ballingurteen	Dunmanway Rural Area	500
Dawros	Kenmare Rural Area	500
Larah South	Cavan Rural Area	500
Barrack Village	New Ross Rural Area	100
Cappard	Gort Rural Area	100
Glenco	Belmullet Rural Area	100

Census 2002. If one person had moved from Castle C, Limerick City to Burgage, Baltinglass, both would also have had populations of 1,000.

INTRIGUING IRISH PLACENAMES

Placename	*From Gaelic*	*Meaning*
Anascual	Abhainn an Scail	River of the phantom
Ardingarry	Ard an Ghaire	Height of shouting
Ballinruan	Baile an Ruáin	Home of the mystery
Bohacogram	Both an Chograim	Hut of the whispering
Inchicore	Inse Chór	Island of the snout
Lettergesh	Leitir Geis	Hillside of the taboo
Modreeny	Má Dreimhne	Plain of fury
Tay Lough	Loch Té	Lake of tea
Skiddernagh	Sciodarnách	Place of puddles
Templenakilla	Teampall na Cille	Church of the church

1 Kerry; 2 Donegal; 3 Clare; 4 Kilkenny; 5 Dublin; 6 Galway; 7 Tyrone; 8 Wicklow; 9 Mayo; 10 Kerry.

MOST & LEAST FREQUENTLY-DRAWN LOTTO NUMBERS, 1994-2003

10-20% more often than average	14, 32, 11, 16, 18, 4, 9
5-10% more often than average	1, 21, 24, 10
0-5% more often than average	31, 22, 7, 20, 2, 42
0-3% less often than average	23, 28, 34, 25, 19, 12, 41, 40
3-5% less often than average	17, 3, 30, 15, 35, 13, 6, 36
5-10% less often than average	29, 33, 5, 39, 27, 37, 8
10-20% less often than average	26, 38

14 drawn 15% more often than average; 38, 19% less often than average.

ITEMS LOOTED DURING 1916 RISING

Air Guns	Fruit	Shoes
Bags of Flour	Golf Sticks	Toffee
Boxes of Biscuits	Musical Instruments	Toy Drums
Chocolates	Pipes & Tobacco	Toys in Boxes
Dolls in Boxes	Rockets & Fireworks	Untrimmed Hats

NO MORE MISTER NICE GUY

"If someone turned up, grabbed my children, mutilated or killed them, I'd spend the rest of my life tracking him down and killing him."

— *Chris de Burgh*

"I would love to have somewhere that I would spit on him (Nicholae Ceaucescu). I believe that shooting was too good and too quick for him."

— *Daniel O'Donnell*

WHO WAS IRELAND'S FIRST HEAD OF STATE?

It was	*According to*
James McNeill, first Governor-General	Conor Cruise O'Brien
Cathal Brugha, first Ceann Comhairle	Taoiseach Bertie Ahern
King George V or Douglas Hyde	Ruth Dudley Edwards
King George V	Michael Laffan of UCD
Douglas Hyde, first President	President Mary McAleese
Cathal Brugha, perhaps...	President Mary McAleese
There would have been lots	Spokesperson for President

Historian Ruth Dudley Edwards says Taoiseach's answer is: "Bollocks from all directions... Bertie has heard *of* Irish history but that's about it."

A BRIEF HISTORY OF SELLAFIELD

The UK's first nuclear plant, Windscale, opens in Cumbria.	*1950*
Windscale plutonium powers Britain's first A-Bomb test.	*1952*
Plume of toxic radioactive isotopes spews into atmosphere.	*1957*
Cluster of birth defects along North East coast of Ireland.	*1958*
The name Windscale is dropped. Plant rebranded 'Sellafield'.	*1981*
British authorities admit 1957 fire cause of lingering deaths.	*1987*
Sellafield pigeons classified as 'nuclear waste' by testers.	*1998*
Plant denies leak cover-up. Leak only 'technically' a leak.	*1998*
Plant falsifies safety measurements on fuel shipped to Japan.	*1999*
BNFL denies that reprocessing plant is to close in 2010.	*2003*

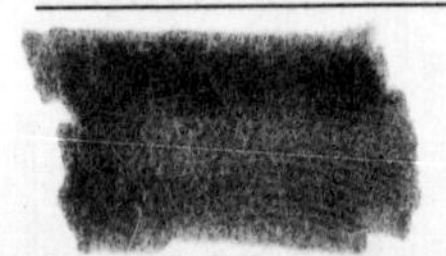

DRINK! FECK! GIRLS!

FATHER JACK'S MOST FREQUENT EXCLAMATIONS

Total times mentioned		*Episodes with most shouts of 'Drink!'*	
Drink!	71	New Jack City (hairy hands)	18
Arse!	8	Tentacles of Doom (holy stone)	13
Feck Off!	8	Hell (caravan holiday)	11
Feck!	6	A Christmassy Ted (Golden Cleric)	11
Girls!	4	Old Grey Whistle Theft (Fr Damo)	4
Gobshite	3	Speed 3 (hairy babies)	4

OTHER WORDS OF WISDOM FROM FATHER JACK

Arse biscuits! Bastard! Brandy! Bras! Curtains! Drink, oh yes! Feckin' water! Feckin' women's knickers! Floor! Get to feck! Gin! Hairy Japanese bastards! Knickers! My arse! Need more drink! Nudie Father Jack! Nuns — reverse! Pub! That would be an ecumenical matter! Thunderbirds! Vodka! Water? Feck! Woman! Yellowpacks!

In published script but not televised: My cock in a burger bun!

ENGLISH WORDS OF GAELIC ORIGIN

Word	*From Gaelic*	*Meaning*
Bard	Bard	Poet
Dig, twig	Tuig	Understand
Galore	Go Leor	Plenty
Kibosh *	Caidhp Báis	Cap of death
Pillion	Pillín	Small pad, cushion
Shanty	Seantigh	Old house
Slob	Slaba	Mud or ooze
Smashing	Is Maith Sin	That is good
Smithereens	Smidiríní	Little bits
Tory **	Tóraí	Pursuer or robber

* The Cap of Death was allegedly a torture used by English soldiers in 1798. It involved putting a bucket or candle of burning pitch on the torturee's head. ** The original Tóraís were pursuers of power.

IT'S RAINING MEN

WHERE TO FIND A MAN IN IRELAND

District	*Area*	*Pop*	*Male*	*%*
Airport	Fingal	269	189	70.3
Cushkillary	Clifden	272	191	70.2
Lackagh	Nenagh	20	14	70.0
Mountheaton	Roscrea	723	504	69.7
Centre A	Cork City	563	369	65.5
Capard	Mountmellick	47	30	63.8
Cherry Orchard A	Dublin	2,177	1,381	63.4
Glenstal	Limerick	916	578	63.1
Eskey	Enniskillen	269	168	62.5
Aughinish	Rathkeale	230	143	62.2

Census 2002. Local electoral divisions.

PEOPLE WHO AUTOMATICALLY ESCAPE JURY DUTY

Ineligible Persons

The President of Ireland.
Judges & ex-judges.
Coroners & deputy coroners.
Attorney General & staff.
The DPP & staff.
Barristers, solicitors & staff.
Court officers, record-takers.
Gardaí Síochána.
Prison officers & staff.
Justice Dept welfare staff.
Forensic scientists.
Members of Defence Forces.
Illiterate, deaf or blind people.
People being medically treated for a mental illness.

Excusable as of Right

TDs and Senators.
Persons in Holy Orders.
Regular priests, ministers etc.
Doctors, dentists, nurses, midwives, vets, chemists.
Heads of Govt Depts.
Civil servants or teachers with cert from boss.
School or college principals.
Whole-time students.
Secretary to Commissioners of Irish Lights.
Masters of vessels, pilots & aircraft commanders.
Persons aged over 65.

DUNPHY ON BIG JACK

Euro 1988	*1992*
"Charlton, using wisely the resources at his disposal, has created one of the world's most formidable football teams. He will now, I think, be remembered as one of the great football managers."	"I think his effect on the game here, on the LOI, schoolboys, junior football etc, will be disastrous. Jack has presided over the creation of a whole culture of playing the game in a certain brutal style that will prove disastrous."

IRISH-BORN BRITISH POETS LAUREATE

Nahum Tate of Dublin was Poet Laureate from 1692-1715. In 1700 he composed his best-known work, 'While Shepherds Watched Their Flocks at Night'.

Cecil Day-Lewis of Laois was Poet Laureate from 1968-1972. He also wrote detective stories as William Blake. His son is the actor Daniel Day-Lewis.

RTE TELEVISION SCHEDULE, 29 SEP 1979

9.30	Pope John Paul II's Arrival at Dublin Airport.
11.30	Papal Mass From The Phoenix Park.
3.30	Liturgy of the Word From Drogheda.
5.30	Children's Shows.
6.00	The Angelus, recited by Pope John Paul II.
6.04	News (with extensive coverage of Papal visit).
6.15	The Pope in Dublin.
8.00	Message to the Sick From Pope John Paul II.
8.05	Nuacht (with extensive coverage of Papal visit).
9.00	News (with extensive coverage of Papal visit).
9.30	The Sacketts (Part 2) Story of a Pioneer Family, with Glenn Ford.
11.15	Late News (extensive coverage of the Papal visit) followed by Closedown.

PAT KENNY'S CHAT

"They have to explain, and if they can't explain they'll have some explaining to do."

On multiple tyre slashings: "It seems to be malicious."

"Heindrich Himmler, arguably the most powerful Nazi leader."

LEAVING CERT SUBJECTS

MOST AND LEAST STUDIED, 2000

Most	*Boys*	*Girls*	*Least*	*Boys*	*Girls*
Maths	100%	100%	Hebrew	1/11250	1/6638
English	99%	99%	Greek	1/3516	1/3516
Irish	97%	97%	Econ History	1/405	1/830
Religion	85%	89%	Agri Economics	1/329	1/663
French	56%	72%	Keyboarding	1/695	1/220

HOW MUCH LONGER WILL YOU LIVE?

Your age now and average Irish lifespan for your birth year			Your age now and average Irish lifespan for your age now			Your age now and how many years you might have to live		
Age	*Male*	*Female*	*Age*	*Male*	*Female*	*Age*	*Male*	*Female*
0	74	80	0	74	80	0	74	80
5	73	79	5	75	80	5	70	75
10	72	78	10	75	80	10	65	70
30	69	74	30	76	81	30	46	51
40	68	72	40	76	81	40	36	41
50	65	57	50	77	81	50	27	31
60	59	61	60	78	82	60	18	22
70	58	59	70	81	84	70	11	14
80	57	58	80	86	88	80	6	8
90	-	-	90	93	94	90	3	4

TAMMANY FÁIL?

Tammany Hall	*Fianna Fáil*
Tammany Hall was a strong political machine, dominated by Irish immigrants in New York.	Fianna Fáil is a strong political machine, founded by a New York immigrant in Ireland.
Tammany Hall was led by 'Boss' Tweed and 'Boss' Croker.	Fianna Fáil was led by CJ Haughey: 'The Boss'.
Tammany Hall was linked in the 1860s to a business-and-politics clique called 'The Ring'.	Fianna Fáil was linked to a business-and-politics clique called 'The Golden Circle'.
Tammany Hall was notorious for charges of double voting.	Haughey's election agent was charged with double voting.
'Boss' Croker spent a month in prison for refusing to give evidence at an 1874 Court case.	Liam Lawlor spent weeks in prison for refusing to give evidence to the Flood Tribunal.
Tammany Hall's influence survived an unwanted coalition of Local Govts in the 1890s.	Fianna Fáil's influence has survived unwanted coalitions with the PDs and Labour.
Before the secret ballot was introduced in 1897, New York voters were aided by Tammany Hall 'shoulder-hitters'.	CJ Haughey held open ballots within Fianna Fáil. Those who dissented "could be intimidated, threatened, even assaulted".*
The influence of Tammany Hall on New York politics finally ended in the 1930s.	In 2003, a FF Cllr proposed that a statue of 'Boss' Croker be erected in Ireland.

* Des O'Malley TD, 1999 Dáil debate: "If you disagreed with the leader's views you could be intimidated, threatened, even assaulted within the precincts of this House by his more thuggish supporters."

THE THIRD SEX

TOILET DOORS, UNIVERSITY COLLEGE CORK, 1980S

1. Men
2. Women
3. Nuns

WHERE ARE THE 'FAIR CITY' CREW?

Monday	*Tuesday*	*Wednesday*
Rehearsals	Studio Filming	Outdoor Filming
Thursday	*Friday*	*Saturday*
Studio Filming	Studio Filming	Rehearsals

SIX PAIRS OF BROTHERS WHO HAVE PLAYED FOOTBALL FOR IRELAND

Brady	Liam & Ray	*O'Brien*	Fran & Ray
Dunne	Tony & Pat	*O'Flanagan*	Kevin & Michael
Moulson	Con & George	*O'Leary*	Dave & Pierce

O'Learys played *together* for Ireland v Bulgaria 1979, N Ireland 1979, Holland 1980. Pierce substituted for Dave v England 1980. Dunnes played together v Spain in Spain 1965, and O'Flanagans did so v England 1946.

VOTE FINE GAEL

"Very few itinerants are actually registered to vote. Those who are, are sometimes exploited by politicians who pay them to vote for them, in some cases by voting illiterately." — *Jimmy Deenihan TD*

"We're going to have to build four houses for every one of the ten homes in the country."
— *John Bruton TD*

"(As FG leader) I am going to electrify the party."
— *Enda Kenny TD*

"America is a good example. They have thousands and thousands of prison places per head of the population."
— *Nora Owen TD*

"In most cases (poverty) is self-induced through gambling or drinking."
— *Brendan McGahon TD*

"Young Fine Gael: Where the Action Is!"
— *Recruitment Slogan*

"The past two referenda have shown that we are not yet a modern sophisticated people. Thank God for that."
— *Alice Glenn TD*

IT'S RAINING WOMEN

Where to find a woman in Ireland

District	*Area*	*Pop*	*Female*	*%*
Gillabbey C	Cork City	1,692	1,091	64.5
Glasheen B	Cork City	734	444	60.5
Dock C	Limerick City	1,059	625	59.0
Rathmines East B	Dublin	5,009	2,902	57.9
Abbey C	Limerick City	625	362	57.9
Tramore A	Cork City	846	489	57.8
Knock South	Claremorris	734	424	57.8
Dock D	Limerick City	1,018	587	57.7
Mardyke	Cork City	885	509	57.5
Pembroke East C	Dublin	3,866	2,212	57.2

Census 2002. Local electoral divisions.

HAPPINESS IN IRELAND, 2002

More Happy	*Less Happy*
Married, live in rural Leinster	Unmarried, live in urban Dublin
Aged under 30 or over 60	Aged between 30 and 60
Have average or higher income	Have lower income
Are healthy and not stressed	Are stressed and not healthy
Feel in control of their lives	Do not feel in control

Amárach Consulting 2002: Quality of Life in Ireland. Note: People with higher incomes are no happier than those with average incomes.

HUGH LEONARD'S PERVY PERCY

In 1971 the Irish film censor banned Hugh Leonard's 'Percy', a saucy British sex comedy. The plot: a man with a penis transplant meets the former sex partners of the organ donor, before reuniting his appendage with the wife of its previous owner.

I SPY: SECRET ASSESSMENTS BY THE US EMBASSY, 1960s-70s

Garret Fitzgerald (FG)
"Would be a brilliant leader in any country."

CJ Haughey (FF)
"Capable, high-powered and ambitious, quite different from run-of-the-mill IRA followers."

Michael O'Leary (Lab)
"His unmarried state does not reflect on his inclinations or opportunities. One of Ireland's most eligible bachelors."

Justin Keating (Lab)
"In 1969 engaged in an anti-apartheid demonstration. Was once a member of the Irish-USSR Society."

Eamon de Valera (FF)
"Lives largely in past. Drinks brandy straight. Likes all food, especially steak, but not fond of ham. Allergic to eggs and mayonnaise."

WHICH IRISH SONGS CAME CLOSEST TO WINNING THE EUROVISION?

Irish Entrant	*Irish Song*	*Irish Score*	*1st Place*	*Irish %*
Linda Martin	*Terminal 3*	137	145	94%
Liam Reilly	*Somewhere in Europe*	132	149	89%
Swarbriggs + 2	*It's Nice to Be in Love Again*	119	136	88%
Sheeba	*Horoscopes*	105	136	77%
Maria Christian	*Wait Until the Weekend Comes*	91	123	74%
Marc Roberts	*Mysterious Woman*	157	227	69%

Years (top to bottom) 1984, 1990, 1977, 1981, 1985, 1997

THREE STAGES OF IRISH HUNGER

Would eat a baby through the bars of a cot
Would eat a farmer's arse through a blackthorn bush
Would eat the leg of the Lamb of God

VICIOUS CIRCLE

"We (The Boomtown Rats) had difficulty getting good enough security to satisfy insurers. Most of the security men in Dublin were so well-known and so violent that their very presence instigated violence." — *Bob Geldof*

THE FIRST & THE 2003 IRISH OPENS

1927			Both at Portmarnock		2003
Player	*Score*	*Prize*	*Player*	*Score*	*Prize*
G Duncan	312	£150	M Campbell	277	€300,000
TH Cotton	313	£90	B Hedblom	277	€156,340
J Smith	315	£60	T Bjorn	277	€156,340
A Compston	317	£50	D Lynn	279	€83,160
W Nolan	319	£40	G Owen	279	€83,160

Total prize fund in 1927 was £750; total prize fund in 2003 was €1,800,000.

"THIS IS WOMEN NOW"

Dáil Eireann, 9 Dec 1993.
Taoiseach, Albert Reynolds:
"On that point, it was stated yesterday… incorrectly as usual, that this commitment was given last Tuesday in the House by the Minister for Justice —"
Fine Gael TD, Nora Owen:
"I said it was given —"
"— The Minister for Justice was ill last Tuesday and was not in the House. No such —"
"— On a point of order —"
"— Excuse me. No such commitment was given —"
"— On a point of order —"
"— Excuse me —"
"— I am calling a point of Order —"
"— when I am speaking, please —"
"I beg your pardon —"
"— The Deputies opposite do not like to hear the truth —"
"— the Ceann Combairle is in charge —"
"— This is women now, you cannot even give way to someone who wants to give you information."

HOW U-TURNS HAPPEN

Charlie McCreevy, Dáil Eireann, 1995

"It has been decreed from the pinnacle of the high moral ground that only Fianna Fáil does political U-turns. All other political parties make policy adjustments in the best interests of the country but never in their own interests, that being the preserve of those uncouth muck savages, unprincipled and power hungry members of Fianna Fáil."

BE CAREFUL OUT THERE

LAWS STILL ON THE STATUTE BOOK

Under S 61 of the Offences Against The Person Act 1861 it is a criminal offence to commit buggery with a cow. Under the Towns Improvement (Ireland) Act 1854 you can be arrested for exposing animals for show or sale in unauthorised places; permitting ferocious dogs go unmuzzled; leading animals on a footpath; throwing rubbish from a house; hanging a clothes line across a street and beating a carpet before 9 am.

LEAST BUSY PRIESTS IN IRELAND

Catholic Diocese	*Catholic Parishioners*	*Active Priests*	*Catholics per Priest*
Kilmore	54,370	90	604
Clonfert	32,600	51	639
Cashel & Emly	78,308	114	687
Achonry	34,405	50	688
Killala	38,001	50	760
Tuam	121,536	147	827
Ferns	98,000	112	875
Ossory	74,519	79	943
Killaloe	109,521	114	961

Catholic Communications Office 2002. Only counts active ministering priests.

PHOBIAS TACKLED ON 'ASK ANNA'

Phobia	*Person*	*Described on show as*
Fear of Flying	Tony Floyd	Dublin window cleaner
Flirting & Dating	Carol O'Connor	Galway woman
Flirting & Dating	Bryan Hogan	Australian divorcé
Fear of Dancing	Norman Newell	Wicklow businessman
Public Speaking	Tom Granville	Best man at a wedding
Driving in Tralee	Maureen Noonan	Dingle woman

MASSACRE AT HIGH NOONAN

THE 30 FINE GAEL TDS WHO DIDN'T RETURN IN 2002

Monica Barnes	Michael J Cosgrave	Charles Flanagan
Sean Barrett	Michael Creed	Brian Hayes
Louis Belton	Austin Currie	Jim Higgins
Andrew Boylan	Michael D'Arcy	*Brendan McGahon*
Paul Bradford	*Austin Deasy*	Jim Mitchell
John Browne	Alan Dukes	Nora Owen
Liam Burke	*Tom Enright*	Gerry Reynolds
Ulick Burke	John Farrelly	Alan Shatter
Donal Carey	Michael Finucane	PJ Sheehan
Deirdre Clune	Frances Fitzgerald	*Ivan Yates*

Eight in italics didn't stand for re-election. Other 22 stood & lost their seats.

THE PLANET ENYA

In 1997 the International Astronomical Union named minor planet number 6433 in honour of Irish singer Enya. The name was proposed by GV Williams. With a 3.96-year elliptical orbit, Enya is between 3 and 7 km wide and between 279.2 and 434.9 million km from the sun. A telescope is required to see Enya as it is 7,000 times less bright than the faintest visible objects.

FIRST TEN IRISH UK NUMBER 1 SINGLES

Softly Softly	Ruby Murray	3 wks	1955
Diane	The Bachelors	1 wk	1964
All Kinds Of Everything	Dana	2 wks	1970
Clair	Gilbert O'Sullivan	2 wks	1972
Get Down	Gilbert O'Sullivan	2 wks	1973
Rat Trap	Boomtown Rats	2 wks	1978
I Don't Like Mondays	Boomtown Rats	4 wks	1979
What's Another Year?	Johnny Logan	2 wks	1980
A Good Heart	Feargal Sharkey	2 wks	1985
Lady In Red	Chris De Burgh	3 wks	1986

THE FUTURE OF IRISH FARMING

Govt Agri-Food 2010 Report	*1998*	*2010*
Viable full-time farmers	44,300	20,000
Part-time farmers	38,500	60,000
Non-viable or micro-farmers	63,500	20,000
Total	146,300	100,000

FAMOUS SAYINGS NEVER SAID

Posterity's Version	*Real Version*
"Publish and be damned." — *Duke of Wellington* (said to blackmailer)	"Write and be damned." — *Duke of Wellington* (note to blackmailer)
"A good footballer, not a great footballer." — *Eamon Dunphy* (about Liam Brady)	"Good footballer, great footballer. I mean, he was never a great footballer." — *Eamon Dunphy*
"That's women for you." — *Albert Reynolds*	"This is women now." — *Albert Reynolds*

Possibly Said: "I had a woman on from Clontarf." — *Joe Duffy*

FIVE-AND-A-HALF DUBLIN LOCALITIES ENDING IN THE LETTER 'O'

1.	Marino	3.	Pimlico	5.	Rialto
2.	Phibsboro	4.	Portobello	5.5	Monto

1911 *Encyclopaedia Britannica* noted Monto's sex trade was "carried out more publicly than even in the South of Europe or Algeria".

MOST ELECTABLE IRISH SURNAMES

BY NUMBER OF TDS ELECTED, 1919-2003

Surname	TDs	Surname	TDs	Surname	TDs
Byrne	13	Gallagher	6	Carter	4
Lynch	12	O'Connor	6	Coughlan	4
Fitzgerald	11	O'Donnell	6	Desmond	4
Murphy	11	O'Malley	6	Esmonde	4
Ryan	11	O'Reilly	6	Finlay	4
Brady	10	Belton	5	Fitzpatrick	4
Brennan	10	Boland	5	Gibbons	4
Burke	10	Connolly	5	Healy	4
O'Sullivan	9	Daly	5	Hughes	4
Ahern	8	Doherty	5	Kennedy	4
Browne	8	Egan	5	Lenihan	4
Collins	8	Fox	5	Maguire	4
Hogan	8	O'Higgins	5	McGrath	4
Crowley	7	O'Keeffe	5	Moloney	4
Hayes	7	O'Leary	5	Moynihan	4
Kelly	7	Reynolds	5	Nolan	4
Walsh	7	Barrett	4	O'Brien	4
Cosgrave	6	Barry	4	O'Donoghue	4
Doyle	6	Blaney	4	Rice	4

The 13 Byrne TDs are Christopher (1921) Alfred & Daniel (1922), Conor (1923), John Joseph (1927), Alfred (1937), Thomas (1951), Patrick (1954), Henry (1965), Hugh (1969), Hugh (1981), Sean (1982) and Eric (1989).

Includes hyphenated names (Healy-Rae=Healy) and close variations of spelling (Ahearn=Ahern).

QUALIFICATIONS TO ENTER MISS IRELAND CONTEST

1. Must be aged 18-25 and at least 5' 7" in stockinged feet.
2. Must "be of good character and possess charm, poise, personality, and beauty of face and figure".
3. Must "never have given birth to a child".
4. Must "never have been through a marriage ceremony, valid or invalid, whether civil, religious or tribal".

WHERE TO MEET A HEATHEN

Most		*Least*	
Dublin City	10.84 %	Monaghan	2.55 %
Galway City	8.63 %	Roscommon	2.81 %
Dun Laoghaire	8.53 %	Longford	2.83 %

Census 2002. Heathens calculated here as those who said they had no religion and those who did not answer the question about religion.

TWO IRISH PLEDGES

"I, (name), in the presence of Almighty God, do solemnly swear allegiance to the Irish Republic, now virtually established, and that I will do my utmost, at every risk, while life lasts, to defend its independence and integrity, and finally, that I will yield implicit obedience in all things, not contrary to the laws of God, to the commands of my superior officers. So help me God! Amen."

— *Fenian Oath, 1859*

"(We) do hereby pledge ourselves in solemn Covenant, throughout this our time of threatened calamity, to stand by one another in defending for ourselves and our children our cherished position of equal citizenship in the United Kingdom, and in using all means which may be found necessary to defeat the present conspiracy to set up a Home Rule Parliament in Ireland... God save the King."

— *Ulster Covenant, 1912*

THE FIRST IRISH FILM CENSOR

James Montgomery was film censor from 1924 to 1940. His philosophy: "I know nothing about films but I do know the Ten Commandments." During his term he banned 1,750 films, compared to 178 banned in Britain. Strongly opposed to "monkey house morality", he installed mirror arcs to his viewing equipment to ensure that he did not miss any fringe glimpses of semi-nudity. His first annual report slammed "indecent dancing" and "the customs of the (international) divorcing classes". He believed that "the real threat to Irish culture is not Anglicisation but Los Angelisation".

TOP THREE ANCESTRIES IN AUSTRALIA

Ancestry	*1986*	*2001*	*Change*	*% of Pop*
Australian	3.4 m	6.7 m	+ 3.3 m	38.7 %
English	6.6 m	6.4 m	- 0.2 m	36.5 %
Irish	0.9 m	1.9 m	+ 1.0 m	11.0 %

Census 2001. Up to 2 ancestries coded per person. Twice as many Irish as next-highest, German. Of every ten Irish-Australians, one is first-generation; two second-generation; seven Australian-born of Australian-born parents.

CJ HAUGHEY — IN HIS OWN WORDS

"You fucking cunt!"
(Hissed at Fintan O'Toole at public function)

At the 1987 Tour de France: "The scene here is the greatest experience of my life!"
Questioner (later): "Wasn't that claim a bit excessive?"
Haughey: "What I said was that it was the greatest experience of my life on the Champs Elysées."

"Get married again."
(To woman seeking rise in widow's pension)

THE NATIONAL ANTHEM

Soldiers are we, whose lives are pledged to Ireland.
Some have come from a land beyond the wave. Sworn to be free,
no more our ancient sireland shall shelter the despot or the slave.
Tonight we man the Bearna Baoghal in Erin's cause, come woe or weal.
'Mid cannon's roar and rifle's peal, we'll sing a soldier's song.

We'll sing a song, a soldier's song, with cheering, rousing chorus, as round our blazing fires we thong, the starry heavens o'er us, impatient for the coming fight, and as we wait the morning's light, here in the silence of the night, we'll sing a soldier's song.	In valley green or towering crag, our fathers fought before us, and conquered 'neath the same old flag that's proudly floating o'er us. We're children of a fighting race, that never yet has known disgrace, and as we march the foe to face, we'll sing a soldier's song.	Sons of the Gael! Men of the Pale! The long watched day is breaking. The serried ranks of Innisfail shall set the tyrant quaking. Our camp fires now are burning low. See in the east a silvery glow. Out yonder waits the Saxon foe, so sing a soldier's song.

ANAGRAMS OF IRISH INFAMY

SELLAFIELD	DEFILES ALL
FATHER MICHAEL CLEARY	*FAMILY? HA! ALERT CRECHE*
MARTIN CAHILL	HALT CRIMINAL

HE SHOOTS... HE RESHOOTS!

In the edition of RTE's 'Fair City' pre-recorded for 31 May 2002, the character Paul assesses Ireland's World Cup chances, saying: "Ah, sure we'll be okay as long as Roy Keane doesn't lose his head." The scene had to be re-shot.

THE SIMPSONS CELEBRATE IRELAND

Homer catches a leprechaun to beat a gypsy curse.

Homer blags into a U2 concert by wearing a green vest, yelling "Potato man!" and delivering a bag of spuds.

One of Bart's chalk lines is 'I did not invent Irish dancing'.

Lisa says angels are a fantasy like unicorns and leprechauns.

Bart discovers that Springfield's 'Whacking Day' was dreamed up "as an excuse to beat up the Irish". An Irishman responds: "But 'twas all in good fun."

St Patrick's Day Parade floats include 'The Drunken Irish Novelists of Springfield' and '2000 Years of Irish Cops'.

Grampa Simpson says he chased the Irish out in 1904.* An Irishman responds: "And a fine job you did, too."

* Jews were chased out of Limerick in 1904

'THE DARK' DAYS OF THE 1960s

John McGahern's *The Dark* was banned in 1965. A primary teacher on leave of absence, he was 'advised' not to return to his job in Clontarf.

When he reported for duty, he was sacked. The Parish Priest said not only had his writing caused trouble, but he had married in a registry office.

When McGahern insisted on a formal letter explaining why he was sacked, the letter read: "Mr McGahern is well aware of the reason of his dismissal."

When he went to his union, the INTO, they declined to help. They told him his membership had lapsed while he was on leave of absence.

An INTO official said they might have helped "if it was just the banned book", but "with marrying this woman, you're an impossible case".

McGahern was asked why he had married an English bride when so many Irish women were "going around with their tongues out for a husband".

FIVE STEPS FROM THE CELTS TO THE TRADITIONAL 32 COUNTIES

APPROX 100 AD

15 main Celtic tribes

Brigantes	Ol nEcmacht
Coriondi	Erainn
Cuala	Gangani
Dal Fiatach	Manaig
Dal Riada (parts of NI & Scotland)	Osraige
	Uaithne
Domnainn	Ulaid
Ebdani	Vellabori

APPROX 600 AD

7 main Kingdoms

Kingdom =	*Today's*
Airgialla	Mid Ulster
Connacht	Connacht
Laigin	Leinster
Munster	Munster
Uí Néill Sth	Meath
Uí Néill Nth	West Ulster
Ulaid	East Ulster

APPROX 1300 AD

11 English-ruled Counties & 5 Great Liberties ruled by Norman Landlords

Counties	Roscommon
Connacht	Tipperary
Cork	Waterford
Dublin	*Liberties*
Kerry	Carlow
Kildare	Kilkenny
Limerick	Trim
Louth	Ulster
Meath	Wexford

Approx a third of island ruled by Gaelic Chieftans

MacCartan	O'Connor
MacCarthy	O'Donnell
MacMahon	O'Farrell
MacMurrough	O'Hanlon
Maguire	O'Neill
O'Brien	O'Reilly

APPROX 1600 AD

English now rule island through 32 Counties

Antrim	Leitrim
Armagh	Limerick
Carlow	Longford
Cavan	Louth
Clare	Mayo
Coleraine	Meath
Cork	Monaghan
Donegal	Queen's Co
Down	Roscommon
Dublin	Sligo
Fermanagh	Tipperary
Galway	Tyrone
Kerry	Waterford
Kildare	Westmeath
Kilkenny	Wexford
King's Co	Wicklow

English Govt renames Co Coleraine as Londonderry.

EARLY 1900S *New Free State Govt renames King's County and Queen's County as Offaly and Laois.*

SOME IRISH SHOWBAND BEN LANG

Ben Lang	=	Slang	from	Ben Lang
Bees	=	Money	from	Bees & Honey
Charlie	=	Party	from	Charlie McCarthy
Rory	=	Door	from	Rory O'Moore
Richard	=	Woman	from	Richard III (=Bird)
Tip	=	Wig	from	Tip & Tig (Tag Game)

IAN PAISLEY'S TOP TEN ENEMIES

1. Roman Catholic Church. "Seed of the serpent... Her clothes reek of the brimstone of the pit. Her words and opinions label her the parrot of Beelzebub, her father."

2. The Pope. "O Father, we can see the great pan-nationalist conspiracy, with the Pope at its head, sending his secret messages to the IRA."

3. Cathal Daly. "The little serpent-like Cardinal with the skin of a snake on his face."

4. Catholic Priests. "We know your church to be the mother of harlots and the abominations of the Earth. Go back to your priestly intolerance, beads, holy water, holy smoke and stink."

5. 'Papishes.' (To Loyalist mob about a Shankill Rd house) "Do you know who is living there? Pope's men, that's who."

6. Vermin. "Unemployment and shortage of houses are due exclusively to the Papist population. They breed like rabbits and multiply like vermin."

7. The European Union. "A beast ridden by the harlot Catholic Church."

8. Queen Mother. Her visit to the Vatican was "spiritual fornication and adultery with the Antichrist".

9. The Ulster Unionist Party. "Judases!"

10. Brian Cowen. "The reason that his lips are so thick is that he was a very disobedient boy and his mother used to put glue on his lips and put him to the floor and keep him there.... If he wants to use his lips to better effect, he should do it somewhere else with people of similar physical looks."

'STAR TREK' REUNIFIES IRELAND

Episode	The Next Generation — The High Ground
Plot	Picard & Crusher captured by rebel leader, Finn
Baddies	Ambiguous. Ruling Rutians are securicrats
Picard	Tells Data that terrorism never achieves its goals
Data	Reminds Picard of Ireland being reunited in 2037
Upshot	The BBC bans the episode as seditious in 1992
Later	BSkyB screen it with offending lines removed

BRITISH ICONS, IRISH CLAIMS

Crown Jewels	Were stolen by an Irishman, Thomas Blood
Downing Street	Named after an Irishman, Charles Downing
Nelson's Pillar	Irish Pillar was built before London Column
Westminster	Roof-slates came from Valencia Island off Kerry
The Union Flag	Made its debut over Dublin Castle in 1801

PARNELL INVENTS BOYCOTTING

Parnell: Now what are you to do with a tenant who bids for a farm from which another tenant has been evicted?

Several Voices: Shoot him!

Parnell: I think I heard someone say 'Shoot him!'.

Crowd: Cheers.

Parnell: I wish to point out to you a very much better way, a more Christian and charitable way, which will give the lost sinner an opportunity of repenting.

Crowd: Laughter. 'Hear, hear!'

Parnell: When a man takes a farm from which another has been evicted you must shun him on the roadside when you meet him; you must shun him in the streets of the town; you must shun him in the shop; you must shun him in the fair green and in the market-place; and even in the place of Worship…

(Ennis, 1880. Up to 90,000 Irish families evicted 1850–1880.)

The tactic was named boycotting after high-profile early victim Captain Boycott.

WHERE TO MEET A CHURCH OF IRELAND MEMBER

Most		*Least*	
Wicklow	7.12 %	Limerick City	1.37 %
Cavan	6.66 %	Cork City	1.53 %
Dun Laoghaire	5.88 %	Louth	1.56 %
Donegal	4.77 %	Roscommon	1.57 %

Census 2002. Dun Laoghaire = Dun Laoghaire-Rathdown.

FANTASY HURLING MATCH

BASED ON SELECTIONS BY JIMMY MAGEE, 1970-2000 V *PRE-1970*

Noel Skehan

Brian Murphy   Pat Hartigan   Brian Corcoran
Brian Whelahan   Mick Roche   Tom Cashman

Frank Cummins   Ger McCarthy

Nicky English   Joe Cooney   Eddie Keher
Jimmy Barry-Murphy   DJ Carey   Eamon Cregan

Christy Ring   Nick Rackard   Jimmy Doyle
Jimmy Langton   Mick Mackey   Liam Devaney

Ned Wheeler   Jack Lynch

Martin Coogan   Pat Stakelum   Jimmy Finn
John Doyle   Nick O'Donnell   Bobbie Rackard

Tony Reddan

Cork: Barry-Murphy, Cashman, Corcoran, Lynch, McCarthy, Murphy, Ring. *Galway:* Cooney. *Kilkenny:* Carey, Coogan, Cummins, Keher, Langton, Skehan. *Limerick:* Cregan, Hartigan, Mackey. *Offaly:* Whelahan. *Tipperary:* Devaney, both Doyles, English, Finn, Reddan, Roche, Stakelum. *Wexford:* O'Donnell, both Rackards, Wheeler.

PROMOTION CHANCES FOR A GARDA

1 Garda in 6 will become a Sergeant.
1 Garda in 40 will become an Inspector.
1 Garda in 70 will become a Superintendent.
1 Garda in 250 will become a Chief Superintendent.
1 Garda in 900 will become a Commissioner.
1 Garda in 11,500 will become Chief Commissioner.

JACK CHARLTON'S FAVOURITE TOPICS

Most Often — *Mentioned in his Autobiography* — *Less Often*

Most Often		Less Often	
Ireland team	68	'Black Book' episode	2
England team	41	Bob Paisley	2
Bobby Charlton	34	The FAI	2
Leeds United	34	Jeff Astle	2
Don Revie	15	1973 FA Cup Final	1
John Aldridge	14	Eamon Dunphy	1
Billy Bremner/Man Utd	13	Orlando	1
M McCarthy/P McGrath	13	Toto Schillaci	1

IN HIPNESS AND IN HEALTH

Dept of Health Website	*Comments Posted by Visitors*
In 2001 the Dept of Health launched a 'Cool Choices' website aimed at early teens. If teens clicked on an icon marked 'Wanna Get High?', they got a list of suggested alternatives to alcohol. These included phone-card collecting, stamp collecting and tying flies for fly-fishing.	"That 'band' (Atomic Kitten) were a very strange choice to promote your cause. They said that they decided on their new member by seeing which applicant could drink the most. Get your act together." "I have many natural highs. One of my most recent ones has been taking the piss out of your site." "My comment: cop the fuck on!"

SHORTEST-NAMED IRISH PLACES

Name	*Area*	*Pop*	*Name*	*Area*	*Pop*
Cur	Oughterard	159	*Nad*	Kanturk	94
Emo	Mountmellick	987	*Moy*	Enistimon	606
Ida	Ida	2,484	*Spa*	Various	280
Lea	Birr	322	*Usk*	Naas	458

Name	*Location*	*Name*	*Location*	*Name*	*Location*
Agha	Carlow	*Deel*	Ballina	*Moat*	Portumna
Ahil	Bantry	*Denn*	Cavan	*Mote*	Roscommon
Anny	Clones	*Doon*	Various	*Muff*	Various
Aran	Glenties	*Drom*	Thurles	*Naas*	Naas area
Ards	Dunfanaghy	*Drum*	Clones	*Naul*	Various
Arva	Various	*Elia*	Roscommon	*Oola*	Tipperary
Ayle	Scarriff	*Emly*	Tipperary	*Owel*	Mullingar
Bawn	Tullamore	*Fews*	Kilmact'mas	*Park*	Waterford
Beal	Listowel	*Ford*	Gorey	*Port*	Newcastle
Bear	Castletown	*Glen*	Various	*Quin*	Tulla
Bert	Athy	*Glin*	Various	*Rath*	Various
Bree	Enniscorthy	*Gort*	Various	*Ring*	Various
Burt	Inishowen	*Inch*	Various	*Rinn*	Mohill
Cams	Roscommon	*Kill*	Various	*Ross*	Various
Carn	Athlone	*Kyle*	Various	*Ruan*	Corrofin
Carn	Bawnboy	*Lack*	Dingle	*Rush*	Various
Colt	Abbeyleix	*Leap*	Various	*Srah*	Birr
Cong	Various	*Lusk*	Fingal	*Tara*	Navan
Coom	Killarney	*Maas*	Glenties	*Trim*	Trim area
Coos	Portumna	*Maum*	Cahirsiveen	*Tuam*	Eniskillen
Corr	Cavan	*Mayo*	Claremorris	*Umma*	Athlone

FIVE IRISH CHART RECORDS

Ireland's first No 1	'She's Not You' by Elvis Presley, 1962
Most weeks at No 1	'Riverdance', eighteen weeks, 1995
Consecutive chart weeks	Ninety: Gloria's 'One Day at a Time'
Most Irish No 1 singles	Seventeen for U2; run began in 1979
Charted in most decades	Joe Dolan: '60s, '70s, '80s, '90s, '00s

FIRST LINES OF IRELAND'S EUROVISION WINNERS

Snowdrops and daffodils, butterflies and bees	1970
I been waiting such a long time looking out for you	1980
Don't, don't close your eyes to how you feel	1987
Sometimes I watch you passing by my window	1992
Showing no emotion, my feelings locked inside	1993
I remember '62, I was sixteen and so were you	1994
I hear your voice on the wind, and I hear you call out my name	1996

Dana, *All Kinds Of Everything;* Johnny Logan, *What's Another Year?;* Johnny Logan, *Hold Me Now;* Linda Martin, *Why Me?;* Niamh Kavanagh, *In Your Eyes;* Harrington & McGettigan, *Rock 'n' Roll Kids;* Eimear Quinn, *The Voice.*

PJ MARA COMES CLEAN, 1980s

Greatest Ambition?	*Biggest Fear?*
"Never to be found out."	"Being found out."

Hot Press, Mad Hatter's Box

THE 'OLD OLD' IRISH BANKNOTES, 1928-1979

Note	*Colour*	*Front*	*Back: (CB)**	*(HL)**	*Last*
10s	Orange	Lady Lavery	Blackwater	Blackwater	1968
£1	Green	Lady Lavery	Unnamed	Lee	1976
£5	Brown	Lady Lavery	Lagan	Lagan	1975
£10	Blue	Lady Lavery	Bann	Bann	1976
£20	Red	Lady Lavery	Boyne	Boyne	1976
£50	Mauve	Lady Lavery	Lee	Shannon	1977
£100	Green	Lady Lavery	Shannon	Erne	1977

Front had picture of lady with harp; model was Lady Kate Lavery. Back had different Irish River God on each note, based on stone heads carved by Edward Smyth for the Custom House, Dublin.

* It is unclear which River God is on some notes. The (CB) list is that of the Central Bank; the (HL) list is that published in 1945 by Harold Leask M Arch MRIA.

UNSUCCESSFUL PETITIONS TO THE STATE'S MILLENNIUM FUND, 1998-99

1. A Liberty-type statue of Jesus or Mary on Howth Head.
2. A National Garda Talent Contest (with regional heats).
3. A National Garda Pilgrimage to Lourdes.
4. An Artistic Exhibition of Used Underwear on Dublin's Ha'penny Bridge (with a booth for public donations).

"AND I'LL BE VERY DIRECT WITH YOU"

MICHAEL D HIGGINS CLARIFIES HIS POSITION ON SECTION 31

"Well, first of all, you know, responsibility for broadcasting has not been transferred to me yet, the order making that transfer has not been made, it will be made in the next few days, that's the reality, and the other point is, of course, that the order precedes me, and it's on the table of the Dáil, and it would take a resolution of the Dáil and so on to change that situation, if one wanted to, because that's another issue, and what I said in my statement, which I issued only two days ago I think, was that I had little enthusiasm for restrictions on broadcasting, and I also had a respect for the complexity of broadcasting issues, and I'll be very direct with you, I said, I say in it, that the question of changing that policy would require very careful consideration, and he proposes to begin the process of consideration without delay; I'm certainly going to evaluate the operation of Section 31, and what I have stated further than that, one of my reasons are, is that, in relation to broadcasting, is a piece of broadcasting legislation the way to set about this, and I can, bluntly, my views haven't changed, that I think it sits uncomfortably in broadcasting legislation, but I'm perfectly open, and I'm not, days before the order is made even transferring broadcasting to me, going to prejudge anything, I am simply going to consider it, and I will consider it, and I'll look to it in its fullest and deepest sense, yes." (RTE, 1993)

"THE MINI-SKIRT, FOR INSTANCE"

Dr Sheehy Skeffington
Censorship of Publications Bill, 1967

"In general, in this Assembly I find the official reporting very accurate, but the other day when I made the point that other things besides literature can arouse sexual passions and I said 'the mini-skirt, for instance', in the first version of the transcript this read 'the Minister for instance'."

WHERE TO POSSIBLY HEAR A CÚPLA FOCAIL

Most		*Least*	
Galway County	40.0 %	Dublin City	21.5 %
Galway City	36.0 %	Louth	23.5 %
Kerry	34.8 %	South Dublin	24.4 %
Mayo	34.1 %	Wexford	24.5 %
Clare	33.5 %	Wicklow	24.6 %

Census 2002. Irish speakers as percentage of population (self-assessed).

FORMER OCCUPATIONS OF NORTHERN IRELAND'S MPs

Gerry Adams	Bartender	M Gildernew	None
Roy Beggs	Vice Principal	M McGuinness	None
David Burnside	PR Man	Eddie McGrady	Accountant
G Campbell	Businessman	Seamus Mallon	Headmaster
Pat Doherty	Site Engineer	Ian Paisley	Moderator
Nigel Dodds	Barrister	Iris Robinson	None
J Donaldson	UDR Member	Peter Robinson	Estate Agent
Sylvia Hermon	Law Lecturer	Martin Smyth	Minister
John Hume	Teacher	David Trimble	Law Lecturer

Dod's Parliamentary Companion 2003. Abbreviated names: Gregory Campbell, Jeffrey Donaldson, Michelle Gildernew, Martin McGuinness.

IRISH BIRTH-YEARS

Most and least common, still living in Ireland 2002

1980	68,716	*1984*	63,314	*1973*	62,680	*<1903*	376
1981	66,648	*1978*	63,176	*1970*	62,197	*1903*	196
1979	65,994	*1983*	62,955	*1975*	62,024	*1904*	303
1982	65,668	*1974*	62,922	*1977*	61,875	*1905*	427
1972	64,566	*1971*	62,906	*1985*	61,834	*1906*	632

Census 2002. Average for 1990s approx 54,500, and for 2000s approx 55,000.
<1903 = born during or before 1902.

SURVIVING THE EASTER RISING CURFEW

Irish Times editorial, 27 April 1916

"What is the fireside citizen to do with those three hours (curfewed, before bedtime)? We can make two or three suggestions. He can cultivate a habit of easy conversation with his family: the years may have made his efforts in this direction spasmodic or laconic. He can put his little garden into a state of decency that will hold promise of beauty. He can do some useful mending and painting about the house. Best of all, perhaps, he can acquire or reacquire the art of reading. Could any better occasion for reading (the works of William Shakespeare) be afforded than the coincidence of enforced domesticity with the poet's tercentenary?"

Dublin Martial Law curfew 7.30pm–5.30am. Shakespeare RIP 1616.

SKIPPED RECORD

A rubbish skip outside the Progressive Democrats' offices in 1997 contained a file of party letters. In one, treasurer Paul Mackay gave party leader Des O'Malley a list of "very loyal supporters" whose appointment to State boards "would make my job easier on the fundraising side".

UNSPORTING FOOTBALL CHANT

"Cross-border bodies with executive powers!
Cross-border bodies with executive powers!"

Chant by Cliftonville fans directed at Linfield fans in wake of 1998 Good Friday Agreement.

THREE NON-FIANNA FÁILERS

DESCRIBED IN THE OIREACHTAS AS 'CUTE HOORS'

Sligo Traveller	*Labour Party*	*All Of Us?*
Got land from council for €1, sold it for €300,000.	"Surprisingly" supported 2nd FF tax amnesty.	"We all had a sneaking regard for the 'cute hoor' culture."
— David Norris, Independent, 2002	— Avril Doyle, Fine Gael, 1993	— Pat Carey, Fianna Fáil, 2000

PROMOTIONAL TAGLINES OF JIM SHERIDAN FILMS

Into the West	Accused of a crime they didn't commit, two city kids and a magical horse are about to become the coolest outlaws ever to ride Into the West.
In the Name of the Father	Falsely accused. Wrongly imprisoned. He fought for justice to clear his father's name.
Some Mother's Son	Between love and loyalty, between life and death, lies a choice no mother should have to make.
The Boxer	Love is always worth fighting for.
Agnes Browne	When Agnes Browne's husband died, she discovered something amazing... Herself.
Borstal Boy	In 1942, acclaimed Irish poet Brendan Behan was sent to a reform school. What he learned was that love knows no prison.

FUN & GAMES WITH THE GAA

1987: Dublin v Cork Semi goes to extra time. Cork team prefer to catch train. Dubs pop a winner into empty net.

1995: Dublin make Charlies of Tyrone in Final: Charlie Redmond dismissed. Plays on for 12 mins. Dubs win.

1998: Clare Hurlers caught short. Beating Offaly by 3 pts with 3 mins left when ref ends game. Replay. Offaly win.

1999: Kerry's Gerard Murphy blasts wide v Tipp. Ball springs back from side-netting. Kerry score on rebound. *Goal!*

THE BUSIEST PRIESTS IN IRELAND

Catholic Diocese	*Catholic Parishioners*	*Active Priests*	*Catholics per Priest*
Dublin	1,041,100	473	2,201
Meath	203,000	113	1,796
Cork & Ross	220,000	123	1,789
Derry	225,353	127	1,774
Kildare & Leighlin	183,105	106	1,727
Armagh	210,342	129	1,631
Down & Connor	312,056	199	1,568
Galway	95,166	66	1,442

Catholic Communications Office, 2002. Only counts active ministering priests.

MALE-DOMINATED BELIEF SYSTEMS

Belief	*Adherents*	*Men*	*%*
Atheist	500	356	71.2
Hindu	3,099	1,970	63.6
Muslim (Islamic)	19,147	11,726	61.2
Agnostic	1,028	626	60.9
No Religion	138,264	82,262	59.5

Census 2002. Methodists are 50:50 men and women.

THE SOUND OF MUSIC

"A socialite is someone who thrives on constant socialism." — Boyzone's Mikey Graham

"Donie Cassidy is the brainchild of my success." — TR Dallas

"We just started playing music because we had an album out with Gael Linn." — Altan's Mairead Ní Mhaonaigh (mis)quoted in *Big Issues*

WHERE TO MEET A METHODIST

Most		*Least*	
Dun Laoghaire	0.57 %	South Tipperary	0.08 %
Donegal	0.48 %	Galway County	0.11 %
Wicklow	0.42 %	Monaghan	0.13 %
Longford	0.32 %	Mayo	0.14 %
Tipperary North	0.31 %	Roscommon	0.16 %

Census 2002.

BEST FANS IN THE WORLD

Glasgow Celtic Social Charter	*Ok2Boo Website*
Celtic seeks "ways to bring people together and create understanding (by) sharing positive values associated with the best in football". Celtic fans should: "Appreciate good skills in football"; "Offer respect to all opponents"; and "Avoid abusive actions and language".	"It is the basic right of any Ireland or Celtic supporter to boo a Rangers player on the basis that he plays for Celtic's nearest and deadliest rivals." It is "perfectly reasonable to whistle at, jeer or boo" Rangers players "at any football match anywhere in the world".

Ok2Boo is a lobby group of "Ireland and Celtic fans". It was set up when the FAI tried to stop sectarian booing of Rangers players at Ireland matches.

RADIO FREE IRELAND, 1916

Media guru Marshall McLuhan noted the Easter Rising rebels' contribution to the evolution of radio. He wrote that 1916 "was the year of the Irish Easter rebellion and of the first radio broadcast. Wireless had already been used on ships as ship-to-shore 'telegraph'. The Irish rebels used a ship's wireless to make, not a point-to-point message, but a diffused broadcast in the hope of getting word out to some ship that would relay their story to the American press."

IRISH SPORTING ANAGRAMS

KEITH WOOD	WE'D HOOK IT
ALEX HURRICANE HIGGINS	*HIGH RELAXING RUINS ACE*
LANSDOWNE ROAD	ADORES OWN LAND

TOP FIVE IRISH WOMEN, 2003

Evening Herald's List			*Ireland on Sunday's List*
Mary Harney	Tánaiste	Singer	Samantha Mumba
Mary Robinson	Ex-President	Singer	Andrea Corr
Susan Denham	Judge	Fundraiser	Caroline Desmond
Moya Doherty	Producer	Fundraiser	Ali Hewson
Maeve Binchy	Writer	Tánaiste	Mary Harney

In 1989 the *Sunday Independent* listed 'Ireland's 20 Most Beautiful Women'. Only 19 were listed, and the cover photo was of Terry Keane, author of the item. On TV, Pat Kenny asked Keane how she felt about "being selected". She said such lists shouldn't be taken too seriously but that it was very nice.

AH GO ON, JOAN

In Father Ted, Mrs Doyle's first name is Joan. It is mentioned only once, in the All Priests Lookalike Show episode.

THE STREETS OF HENRY MOORE, EARL OF DROGHEDA

This 17th Century Dublin city centre landlord liked his name. He named four of his streets Henry St, Moore St, Earl St and Drogheda St (later to be Sackville, then O'Connell St).

To complete the set, he named a lane off Drogheda Street 'Of Lane'. He now owned five streets which collectively read 'Henry' 'Moore', 'Earl' 'Of' 'Drogheda'.

GO DIRECTLY TO JAIL

MOST & LEAST LANDED-ON IRISH MONOPOLY SQUARES

Jail (includes landing on Go to Jail)	*1 in 16*
Henry Street	*1 in 31*
Go, Heuston Station, Westmoreland Street	*1 in 32*
Busaras	*1 in 33*
Dublin Airport, Pearse Street, Free Parking	*1 in 34*
Dame & Abbey Streets, Waterworks	*1 in 36*
Dawson, Capel, Talbot, North Earl & George's Streets	*1 in 37*
Electric Company, O'Connell & Wicklow Streets	*1 in 38*
Shrewsbury Road, Community Chest 2 *	*1 in 38*
Nassau & Grafton Streets	*1 in 40*
Kildare Street, Shannon Airport, Community Chest 3 *	*1 in 42*
Rathgar, South Circular, Rathmines, Income Tax	*1 in 43*
Kimmage, Ailesbury Road, Super Tax	*1 in 45*
Crumlin	*1 in 48*
Community Chest 1 *	*1 in 53*
Chance 2 *	*1 in 100*
Chance 1 & 3 *	*1 in 111*

* When Community Chest or Chance cards send you to another square, it is counted here as landing directly on the square that you have been sent to.

Based on a computer analysis of probabilities by Jim d'Ambrosia. You will land more often on squares that you can be sent to, such as Jail and Go, and on squares soon after them.

TWENTY PRIESTS IN 'FATHER TED'

Father		*Father*	
Ted Crilly	Our Hero	*Liam Finnegan*	Dancing
Dougal Maguire	Ah, Right	*Noel Furlong*	Youth Club
Jack Hackett	Drink!	*Jose Hernandez*	Cuban
Dick Byrne	Rugged Island	*Damo Lennon*	Gurrier
Buzz Cagney	Californian	*Cyril McDuff*	Rugged Island
Liam Deliverance	Lovely Girls	*Billy O'Dwyer*	DJ Gambler
Larry Duff	Mobile Phone	*Austin Purcell*	Boring
Barty Dunne	Laughing	*Fintan Stack*	Jungle Music
Jim Johnson	Rugged Island	*Paul Stone*	No, I'm Fine
Fintan Fay	Monkey	*Todd Unctious*	Thief

IRISH TWO-PERSON HOUSEHOLDS

Husband & wife	169,668	Lone father & child	10,813
Lone mother & child	57,499	Two related persons	28,251
Cohabiting couple	41,751	Non-related persons	25,718

Census 2002.

TEN YOUNGEST CURRENT TDs

AND WHETHER THEIR FATHER WAS ALSO A TD

Name	*Age*	*Party*	*Constituency*	*Father*
Damien English	24	FG	Meath	No
Olwyn Enright	27	FG	Laois Offaly	Yes
Niall Blaney	28	Ind	Donegal North East	Yes
Denis Naughten	28	FG	Longford Roscommon	Yes
Paul Kehoe	29	FG	Wexford	No
Simon Coveney	29	FG	Cork South Central	Yes
Mildred Fox	30	Ind	Wicklow	Yes
Paul Gogarty	33	GP	Dublin Mid West	No
Cecilia Keaveney	33	FF	Donegal North East	Yes
Tom McEllistrim	33	FF	Kerry North	Yes

Age at date elected, May 2002.

HOW JACK CHARLTON BECAME IRISH FOOTBALL MANAGER

DESPITE GETTING ONLY 3 VOTES OUT OF 18 AT THE FAI

The Shortlist: Amidst flurry of media speculation, two FAI men drive around England in a hired car seeking suitable candidates. Final shortlist is declared unchangeable: Jack Charlton, Manchester City boss Billy McNeill and Irish youth manager Liam Tuohy.

The Politics: Former Irish boss John Giles has declined to enter race. Then the Man City board refuses to let McNeill apply. FAI man tells Giles he would get the job if he applied. Giles is now a candidate — but only if the FAI agree to change the 'unchangeable' shortlist.

The Plan: After heated debate, 18-man FAI Executive agrees to add Giles to the shortlist. Then, with this precedent set, President Des Casey springs a new surprise candidate: former Liverpool boss Bob Paisley. Paisley can win with 9–9 tie, as Casey has casting vote.

The Vote: Paisley gets the necessary 9 votes; Charlton, Giles and Tuohy 3 each. After a side vote eliminates Tuohy, the next vote is Paisley 9, Charlton 5, Giles 4. Then, with Giles gone, one Paisley voter switches, upsetting the plan. Charlton wins by 10-8.

The Aftermath: Months after interviewing him in a motorway café, the FAI couldn't find Charlton to offer him the job. Charlton's friend Jimmy Armfield rang him: "Congratulations on getting the job, Jack." "What job?" "Manager of Ireland." "Oh. I'd forgotten about that."

IRELAND'S LONGEST EVER HEADLINE?

NINE MONTHS' JAIL FOR WOMAN
WHO SET AN ALSATIAN DOG ON SERGEANT
AND EXPOSED HER BREASTS AND
'MOONED' HER BOTTOM AT GARDAI

— *Waterford News & Star*

CLASSIC PUBLIC INFORMATION CAMPAIGNS

Mr Careless Goes to Town	1940s motor safety film
Safe Cycling	1940s safe cycling film
Good Manners In Church	1960s Catholic information film
The Safe Cross Code	1970s road safety for children
Smash the Round System	1970s anti-excessive drinking
Messing with the Kids *	1970s with Fr Brian D'Arcy
Just the Two Will Do	1980s anti-drink-driving
Phone Wreckers are Idiots	1980s with Bob Geldof

* Fr D'Arcy calmed parental fears about rock music.

WHERE TO MEET A CATHOLIC

Most			*Least*
Roscommon	94.1 %	Dun Laoghaire	81.5 %
Mayo	93.1 %	Dublin City	82.2 %
Tipperary South	92.8 %	Wicklow	82.8 %
Limerick County	92.8 %	Galway City	85.5 %
Galway County	92.8 %	Donegal	86.6 %

Census 2002.

YOURS IN CONFIDENCE

Paedophile Smear: In April 2003 the *Observer's* Henry McDonald published a secret 1999 Ministerial briefing paper about sex abuse in orphanages and industrial schools. The document labelled *victims* of these crimes as dysfunctional potential paedophiles who were a danger to their own and other people's children.

Telephone Records: In April 2002 the Govt confidentially instructed telecommunications operators to store traffic information for at least three years about every phone, fax and mobile call, and not to tell their customers about it. The scheme was revealed a year later by Karlin Lillington in the *Irish Times*.

ASK ABOUT GARDENING

"I'm not telling you how (my prize leeks) got to be that size. It's secret. But what I will tell you is that you have to think like a vegetable." — Michael Walton

"And now we come to the dahlia, a plant that you either love or hate. I haven't made up my mind which." — Thelma Mansfield

Caller: "I've a problem with my garden. It's overgrown with mallow."
Gerry Daly: "Tree mallow?"
Caller: "No, there's about eight."

TOP IRISH BOX-OFFICE HITS, 1996-2003

2003	Veronica Guerin	Star Wars Episode 1	*1999*
2002	Spiderman	Titanic	*1998*
2001	Bridget Jones' Diary	The Full Monty	*1997*
2000	Gladiator	Michael Collins	*1996*

COMINATCHA!

2FM'S OPENING SCHEDULE, AS RADIO 2, 31 MAY 1979

12.30 pm: 'On The Air'. Padraig Faulkner, the Min for Posts & Telegraphs, launches Ireland's second national radio service.

12.35 pm: 'Pop Around Ireland', an afternoon musical greetings show. Programme opens with Boomtown Rats hit 'Like Clockwork'.

5 pm: 'Wheelin' Home' with Marty Whelan.

7 pm: 'The Heather Breeze'. Trad & Folk with Áine Hensey.

8 pm: 'Keep it Country' with Pascal Mooney.

10 pm: 'Night Moves' with Mark Cagney.

12 pm: 'Dave Fanning Rocks'.

2 am: Closedown.

RECREATIONAL ACTIVITIES OF NORTHERN IRELAND'S MPs

Gerry Adams	Gaelic sports, Irish traditional music	SF
Roy Beggs	Fishing	UUP
David Burnside	Fishing, Shooting, Motor cycling	UUP
G Campbell	Football, Music, Reading	DUP
Pat Doherty	Walking, Reading, Building stone walls	SF
Nigel Dodds	None	DUP
J Donaldson	Hill-walking, Reading, Church	UUP
Sylvia Hermon	Fitness, Swimming, Ornithology	UUP
John Hume	None	SDLP
M Gildernew	None	SF
M McGuinness	Cooking, Walking, Reading, Fly-fishing	SF
Eddie McGrady	Walking, Gardening	SDLP
Seamus Mallon	Angling, Horseracing, Golf	SDLP
Ian Paisley	History, Antiquarian book collecting	DUP
Iris Robinson	Interior design	DUP
Peter Robinson	Golf, Bowling, Breeding koi carp	DUP
Martin Smyth	Travel, Photography, Reading	UUP
David Trimble	Music, Reading	UUP

Source: Dod's Parliamentary Companion 2003. Ian Paisley has a collection of 18,000 books. Abbreviated names: Gregory Campbell, Jeffrey Donaldson, Michelle Gildernew, Martin McGuinness.

IRISH WISDOM

I have never seen a situation so dismal that a policeman couldn't make it worse. — Brendan Behan

Outside every thin woman is a fat man trying to get in. — Sean Mac Reamoinn

A man once said to me that he was an atheist, but on purely rational grounds. If there is no God, he said, the thing (blasphemy) is stupid and unnecessary. If there is, it is dangerous. — Flann O'Brien

YOU'RE TUNED TO RADIO HITLER

What? During World War II, a Berlin radio station broadcast Nazi propaganda into Ireland, promising Irish unity.

Who? Fluent Irish speaker Hans Hartmann; Lord Haw-Haw William Joyce; future Aosdána tSaoi Francis Stuart.

Irish Govt Protests: Only two: when Stuart condemned IRA man's execution, and advised listeners to oppose Fine Gael.

Later: At war's end, President de Valera 'neutrally' visited the German Embassy to offer his condolences on Hitler's death.

NICKNAMES OF DUBLIN LANDMARKS

The Dick with the Stick	James Joyce, Earl Street
The Fag on the Crag	Oscar Wilde, Merrion Square
The Floozy in the Jacuzzi	Formerly of O'Connell Street
The Stiletto in the Ghetto *	Currently of O'Connell Street
The Flue with the View	Smithfield Chimney
The Hags with the Bags	Beside Ha'penny Bridge
The Tart with the Cart	Molly Malone, Grafton Street

* Song title for the Spire: I Can See Clerys Now the Crane Has Gone.

WE DON'T WANT TO GIVE YOU THAT

TWO TRICKY QUESTIONS ASKED ON RTE'S 'WHO WANTS TO BE A MILLIONAIRE?'

Q. A brown statue of an Irish writer and statesman stands in front of Trinity College in Dublin. Is it: (a) Oliver St John Gogarty, (b) Thomas Moore, (c) Thomas Davis or (d) Sir Edmund Burke?

A. *Statues of both Davis and Burke stand in front of TCD.*

Q. Where in the human body is the lunula located? Is it: (a) the heart, (b) the fingernail, (c) the eye or (d) the ear?

A. *It is a feature of both the heart and the fingernail.*

BERTIE AHERN — WHITE ELEPHANT HUNTER

"I don't think it helps people to start throwing white elephants and red herrings at each other."

"I've never met a socialist in my life and if I do I'll tell you."

"I can't say I have met any homosexuals."

"There have been disputes between fractions."

"Charles J Haughey wanted to transform Temple Bar into Ireland's West Bank."

"There's been no cuts. There's been a moderation in the increases."

"I think Charlie Haughey is basically a very good man and unfortunately he got into things like the lifestyle, and the bills caused him to do some things that I feel very strongly about."

DOWN OUR WAY

WHERE DO MOST AND LEAST PEOPLE LIVE IN IRELAND?

Most		*Least*	
Dublin Region	1,110,600	Arigna, Manorhamilton	15
Dublin City	495,101	Ballynaneashagh, Waterford	17
Cork City/County	448,181	Lackagh, Nenagh	20
Cork County	324,843	Sheskin, Belmullet	25
South Dublin	239,887	Whiddy, Bantry	29
Galway	208,826	Tircahan, Bawnboy	32
Fingal	196,223	Ballaghassaan, Edenderry	34
Dun Laoghaire	191,389	Loughatorick, Loughrea	34
Limerick	175,529	Teebane, Enniskillen	34
Kildare	163,995	Newgrove, Granard	37

Census 2002.

BEGORRAH, PADDY

Three in every ten TDs elected since 1922 have been named some variation of Paddy, Mick, Seán or Seamus.

CHURCH & STATE CORRESPONDENCE ABOUT 'MOTHER & CHILD' SCHEME

Dr Noel Browne was forced to resign as Health Minister in 1951 when medics spurred the Catholic Hierarchy to oppose a new free health care scheme. The Hierarchy, Taoiseach John A Costello and Seán MacBride (Browne's Clann Na Poblachta leader) all put pen to paper.

Bishops to Taoiseach: "Doctors trained in institutions in which we have no confidence may be appointed as medical officers under the proposed services, and may give gynaecological care not in accordance with Catholic principles..." (10 Oct 1950)

Taoiseach to Browne: "You do not appear to realise the serious implications... as you have continued to publicise the scheme to which objections have been taken. Such action might well seem to be defiance of The Hierarchy..." (15 Mar 1951)

Taoiseach to Bishops: "His Grace of Dublin has kindly agreed to inform the Standing Committee that the Government would readily and immediately acquiesce in a decision of The Hierarchy concerning faith or morals... " (27 Mar 1951)

Bishops to Taoiseach: "The Hierarchy cannot approve of any scheme which must foster undue control by the State in a sphere so delicate and so intimately concerned with morals as that which deals with gynaecology or obstetrics..." (5 Apr 1951)

MacBride to Browne: "A situation where it is made to appear that a conflict exists between the spiritual and temporal authorities is always undesirable; in the case of Ireland it is highly damaging to the cause of national unity..." (10 Apr 1951)

THE £34,000 QUESTION

Six quick-fire questions sprung by RTE on a Fianna Fáil hopeful in the 1998 Cork South Central By-Election.

Q: Who was the first TD elected to Cork SC in the general election?
A: *Don't know.*

Q: What paramilitary organisation has not yet declared a ceasefire?
A: *Don't know.*

Q: How many in Cork city are unemployed to the nearest thousand?
A: *Don't know.*

Q: How many joyriders were killed in Cork this year?
A: *About fourteen.*

Q: Name the Ceann Comhairle and Leas Cheann Comhairle.
A: *Don't know.*

Q: What salary does a TD earn?
A: *About £34,000.* (Correct answer.)

IRISH LITERARY ANAGRAMS

SEAN O'CASEY	ACE ON ESSAY
WILLIAM BUTLER YEATS	*I'M REALLY A SUBTLE WIT*
OSCAR WILDE	I LACE WORDS

CEOL AN GHRÁ, 1972

IRELAND'S ONLY IRISH-LANGUAGE EUROVISION ENTRY

Éistigí! Éistigí! Cloisim arís é, ceol an ghrá.
'Seo nó ansúid dom, bíonn sé de shíor liom, ceol an ghrá.
I lár na cathrach breá, cois abhainn nó é trá,
Cloisim an tiún, is tú mo rún, sin ceol an ghrá...

Performed by Sandie Jones. Written by Joe Burkett and Liam Mac Uistin. Finished 15th. UK entry was New Seekers' 'Beg, Steal or Borrow'. Luxembourg's Vicki Leondras won with 'Apres Toi'.

"WHAT'S THAT WORD?"

RODDY COLLINS DESCRIBES WOMEN'S FOOTBALL

"I think it's, eh, what's that word? Em, it's not normal.
What's that word? It's not normal, what do you call it?
It's, eh… Aaaah, what's that bleedin' word?
You know when something's like, like, em…
A freak show! I think it's a freak show."

(Roddy Collins managed Bohemians' double-winning team of 2001.)

WHERE TO MEET A PRESBYTERIAN

Most		*Least*	
Monaghan	4.64 %	Offaly	0.11 %
Donegal	4.20 %	Limerick City	0.13 %
Cavan	1.36 %	Limerick County	0.13 %
Dun Laoghaire	0.75 %	Roscommon	0.13 %
Wicklow	0.51 %	North Tipperary	0.14 %

Census 2002.

RANKS OF THE IRISH DEFENCE FORCES

Lieutenant-General	1	Battalion QM-Sergeant	51
Major-General	3	Company Sergeant	248
Brigadier-General	8	Company QM-Sergeant	258
Colonel	37	Sergeant	1,291
Lieutenant-Colonel	131	Corporal	2,089
Commandant	440	Private	5,296
Captain	355	Cadet	108
Lieutenant	174	Reserve of Officers	179
Second Lieutenant	94	Reserve of Men	287
Sergeant Major	48	Second Line Reserve	12,631

The ranks from Lieutenant-General to Second Lieutenant are Commissioned Officers. All other ranks except Reserves are Non-Commissioned Officers. QM-Sergeant = Quartermaster-Sergeant. CSO 2002.

JAILED FOR CORRUPTION

Without any tribunals, on 13 March 1931, two Tipperary Councillors were convicted in Court of taking £20 for procuring a Council cottage. Imposing on them six months in jail and a seven-year ban from public office, the Judge remarked that "Public figures should not abuse their trust".

IRELAND'S CLEANEST & DIRTIEST URBAN CENTRES, 2003

The Cleanest		*The Dirtiest*	
Cavan Town	Cavan	Sligo Town	Sligo
Kilrush	Clare	Swords	Fingal
Fermoy	Cork	Galway City	Galway
Dun Laoghaire	DL-R	Wexford Town	Wexford
Clonmel	Tipperary	Navan	Meath
Kilkenny City	Kilkenny	Dublin City Centre	Dublin
Tralee	Kerry	Tullamore	Offaly

Irish Businesses Against Litter, June 2003. DL-R=Dun Laoghaire-Rathdown.

ADVERTISING CLASSICS

The two infallible powers: the Pope and Bovril. — *Bovril* (late 1800s)

Three doctors out of every four use gas fires. — *Dublin Gas* (1930s)

A maid for every room. — Ad for electricity, *ESB* (1930s)

The best thing about listening to Dave Fanning is you can't see him. — *Big D Radio* (1970s)

Dr White's Panty Pads. Lil-lets. Big bonus offer on leading brands. But hurry! This bonus offer is for a limited period only. — Trade advert, *Checkout Mag* (1970s)

There is a peculiar thing between myself and my typewriter… — Kevin Myers, *Irish Times* (1980s)

THE MAGICAL CITIES OF TÍR NA NÓG

City	*Druid*	*Treasure Given to Newly-arriving Gods*
Falias	Morfesa	'Lia Fáil', The Stone of Destiny
Gorias	Esras	'Freagarthach', The Sword of Nuada
Murias	Semias	'Gae Assail', The Spear of Lugh
Findias	Uiscias	The Cauldron of Dagda

The Gods of the Tuatha dé Dannan lived in Tír Na nÓg.

FANTASY GAA FOOTBALL MATCH

BASED ON SELECTIONS BY JIMMY MAGEE, 1970-2000 V *PRE-1970*

Billy Morgan

Bobby O'Malley   John O'Keeffe   Robbie Kelleher
Páidí Ó Sé   Kevin Moran   Paudie Lynch

Jack O'Shea   Brian Mullins

Matt Connor   Larry Tompkins   Pat Spillane
Mikey Sheehy   Jimmy Keaveney   Peter Canavan

Kevin Heffernan   Tom Langan   Paddy Doherty
Packie McGarty   Seán Purcell   Seán O'Neill

Jim McKeever   Mick O'Connell

Stephen White   John Joe O'Reilly   Seán Murphy
Seán Flanagan   Eddie Boyle   Enda Colleran

Dan O'Keeffe

Cavan: O'Reilly. *Cork:* Morgan, Tompkins. *Derry:* McKeever. *Down:* Doherty, O'Neill. *Dublin:* Heffernan, Kelleher, Moran, Mullins, Keaveney. *Galway:* Colleran, Purcell. *Kerry:* Lynch, Murphy, O'Connell, both O'Keeffes, Ó Sé, O'Shea, Sheehy, Spillane. *Leitrim:* McGarty. *Louth:* Boyle, White. *Mayo:* Flanagan, Langan. *Meath:* O'Malley. *Offaly:* Connor. *Tyrone:* Canavan.

THE COMMITTEE ON EVIL LITERATURE, 1926

TWENTY 'OBJECTIONABLE' PUBLICATIONS SUBMITTED BY THE CHRISTIAN BROTHERS

Answers Library
Betty's Paper
Bits Of Fun
Dainty Novels
Eve's Own Stories
Girl's Companion
Home Companion
Illustrated Police News
Lloyd's Weekly News
London Life & Society
News of the World
Peg's Paper & Companion
The People
Sporting Times (Pink 'Un)
Thompson's Weekly News
Vogue
The Winning Post
Woman's Life
Woman's Weekly
Woman's World

Under public pressure, Justice Min Kevin O'Higgins established this Committee in 1926 to report on the need for more censorship.

THE LIGHTER SIDE OF LEADING FINE GAEL

Enda Kenny in 2002 joked about a Moroccan barman with "shiny teeth" calling African leader Patrice Lumumba "some nigger killed in the war". He apologised after a newspaper published the joke.

Michael Noonan in 2002 led a party of fiscal rectitude that offered State compensation to taxi drivers and stock market losers. When canvassing in Roscommon, he was hit in the face with a custard pie.

John Bruton told a reporter in 1995 that he was "sick of answering questions about the fucking peace process". Later he joked at an RTE-free event "at least I won't be asked about the fucking peace process".

Alan Dukes was upset in 1988 when ex-Junior Minister John Donnellan predicted that "If it was raining soup, Dukes would have a fork in his hand". He quickly had Donnellan expelled from the Parliamentary Party.

FICTIONAL AMERICAN TV CHARACTERS WHO ARE IRISH OR IRISH-AMERICAN

Character	Role	Show	Decade
Doyle	Angel	Angel	1990s
Monica	Angel	Touched by an Angel	1990s
Jack McCoy	Asst DA	Law & Order	1990s
Miles O'Brien	Officer	Star Trek	1990s
Christine Cagney	Detective	Cagney & Lacey	1980s
Sam Malone	Bar Owner	Cheers	1980s
Mindy McConnell	Friend	Mork & Mindy	1970s
Shirley Feeney	Friend	Laverne & Shirley	1970s
Steven Kiely	Doctor	Marcus Welby MD	1970s
Mike Brady	Father	The Brady Bunch	1970s
Steve McGarrett	Policeman	Hawaii Five-O	1970s
Frank McNeill	Police Chief	Kojak	1970s
Trapper McIntyre	Surgeon	M*A*S*H	1970s
Hot Lips Houlihan	Nurse	M*A*S*H	1970s
Francis Mulcahy	Chaplain	M*A*S*H	1970s
Radar O'Reilly	Clerk	M*A*S*H	1970s
Finnegan	Villian	Star Trek	1960s
Kevin Reilly	Relief Staff	Star Trek	1960s
Willie Gilligan	First Mate	Gilligan's Island	1960s
Francis Muldoon	Policeman	Car 54 Where Are You?	1960s
Flint McCullough	Scout	Wagon Train	1960s
Chief O'Hara	Police Chief	Batman	1960s
Micky Mulligan	Studio Page	Micky Rooney Show	1950s

THE UNFAIR SEX

"There is no point sending in men to do that type of work. It should be a woman's job."— Councillor *Joe O'Shea* of Fianna Fáil, debating who should clean Tramore's public toilets.

"Divorced wives are not an attractive proposition on the marriage market if they have a number of children in tow."— *Rory O'Hanlon*, Judge and chairman of the No Divorce campaign.

TREATS FROM THE 1960s & 1970s

Broken Chocolate	Gobstoppers	Ninety Nines
Bulls Eyes	Ice Cream Wafers	Peggy's Legs
Fizzle Sticks	Liquorice Snakes	Penny Bars

PARLIAMENTARY LANGUAGE

TERMS OF DISDAIN USED IN THE OIREACHTAS, 1919-2003

Term	*Frequency*	*Last Used By*		*When*
Foolish	5741 times	Michael McDowell	PD	Mar 03
Childish	749 times	Michael McDowell	PD	Feb 03
Idiotic	627 times	Brian O'Shea	Lab	Feb 03
Coward	255 times	Mary O'Rourke	FF	Nov 01
Twit	242 times	Michael D Higgins	Lab	Feb 02
Clown	157 times	Johnny Brady	FF	Dec 02
Crackpot	109 times	Joan Burton	Lab	Nov 02
Cute Hoor	16 times	David Norris	Ind	Dec 01
Muppet	13 times	Michael McDowell	PD	Nov 02
Gobshite	2 times	Brendan McGahon *	FG	Feb 97

* Twice

2FM'S TOP 30 MUSICAL SUPERSTARS, EVER!

1	Elvis Presley	11	Neil Diamond	21	Abba
2	The Beatles	12	The Bee Gees	22	Cliff Richard
3	Stevie Wonder	13	Chicago	23	Garth Brooks
4	Rolling Stones	14	Four Seasons	24	Cher
5	Elton John	15	Hall and Oates	25	Beach Boys
6	Marvin Gaye	16	Diana Ross	26	Lionel Richie
7	The Shadows	17	Billy Joel	27	Fleetwood Mac
8	Paul McCartney	18	Madonna	28	David Bowie
9	Aretha Franklin	19	The Jacksons	29	Donna Summer
10	The Supremes	20	U2	30	Michael Jackson

From Top 100 Superstars, broadcast 1 April 2002. Selected by 2FM staff.

THE CAST OF WANDERLY WAGON

O'Brien	Tuck-scoffing scaredy-cat	Eugene Lambert
Godmother	Traditional Irish mammy	Nora O'Mahoney
Rory	The wagon's first driver	Bill Goulding
Pádraig	The horse	Himself
Judge	O'Brien's faithful dog	Himself
Crow	Caw! Caw! Caw! Caw!	Himself
Fox	Surprisingly, a fox	Himself
Forty-Coats	Sartorial superfluity	Fran Dempsey
Dr Astro	An evil villain	Frank Kelly
Sneaky Snake	Dr Astro's sidekick	Himself

RTE's Pre-Muppets Doctor Who, 1968-1981. First 'Pádraig' died series 1.

20 IRISH POSTAGE STAMPS, 2002-03

Soccer Legends	*Fauna & Flora*	*Rock Legends*
Roy Keane	7-Spotted Lady-bird	Phil Lynott
Paul McGrath	Leaf Beetle	Rory Gallagher
David O'Leary	Great Diving Beetle	Van Morrison
Packie Bonnar	Green Tiger Beetle	U2

Paintings from National Gallery		*Individual Stamps*
Jack B Yeats	'Before the Start'	King Brian Boru
Jules Breton	'The Gleaners'	Archbishop Croke
Giovanni Panini	'The Colosseum'	Frank O'Connor
Nathaniel Hone	'The Conjuror'	Saint Padre Pio

MARY HARNEY'S IRISH JOKE

"I've good news and bad news, which do you want first?"
"The bad news."
"The English have landed on the moon."
"Jaysus, we'll never hear the end of it. What's the good news?"
"All of them."
(Delivered at a 2002 Conference)

POPULATION OF IRELAND 2001-02

USING THE TRADITIONAL 32 COUNTIES & 4 PROVINCES

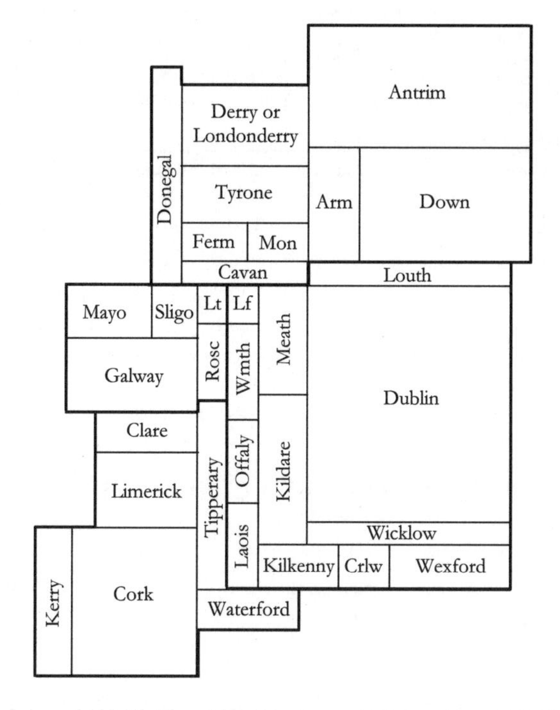

Leinster 2,105,449; Ulster 1,931,838; Munster 1,101,266; Connacht 464,050

Arm Armagh, *Crlw* Carlow, *Ferm* Fermanagh, *Lf* Longford, *Lt* Leitrim, *Mon* Monaghan, *Rosc* Roscommon, *Wmth* Westmeath

BESTSELLING IRISH NEWSPAPERS 1973

Sunday Press	407,000	*Evening Herald*	138,000
Sunday Independent	322,000	*Irish Press*	96,000
Irish Independent	166,000	*Cork Examiner*	60,000
Evening Press	139,000	*Irish Times*	60,000

GOOOOOD *MORNING IRELAND!*

"From me, Richard Crowley … No … From Richard Crowley and me, Brian Dobson, good morning."
— *'Confused' of Montrose*

"Zidane will be given a house with a swimming pool and a gardener thrown in."
— *Reporter*

"Anyone in a panic because I said it's 16 minutes to 8 should know it's 16 minutes *past* 8 … The time is now coming up to 17 minutes to 8."
— *Cathal McCoille*

"A natural father should have the right to object to the adoption of his child. I beg your pardon, his or *her* child."
— *Contributor*

"A police force should be above the suspicion of Caesar's wife."
— *Presenter*

"That gives a swing of over 20% against the incumbent. Of course, he's not the incumbent anymore. Unfortunately, he's dead."
— *David Hanly*

WHERE TO FIND A CINEMA SEAT

Most	*Screens*	*Seats*	*Least*	*Screens*	*Seats*
Dublin	89	20,686	Leitrim	2	235
Cork	40	7,077	Carlow	3	520
Limerick	19	4,390	Kildare	5	628

NI: *Most* Antrim 86 screens and 18,044 seats; *Least* Fermanagh 7 and 1,181.

PLUCKY IRISH WORLD RECORDS

World's Fastest One-Mile Speed March with a 40-lb Pack

Paddy Doyle
5 mins 35 secs
Ballycotton, 7 Mar 1993

World's Fastest Time to Pluck a Turkey

Vincent Pilkington
1 min 30 secs
Cootehill, 17 Nov 1980

POPULATION OF ISLAND 2001-02

USING CURRENT COUNTIES, CITIES AND NI DISTRICTS

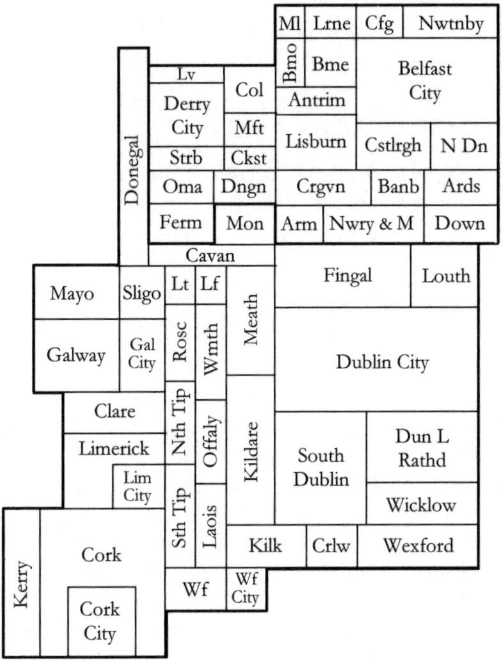

Ml Lrne Cfg Nwtnby
Bmo Bme Belfast City
Lv Col
Derry City Antrim
Mft Lisburn Cstlrgh N Dn
Donegal Strb Ckst
Oma Dngn Crgvn Banb Ards
Ferm Mon Arm Nwry & M Down
Cavan
Mayo Sligo Lt Lf Meath Fingal Louth
Galway Gal City Rosc Wmth Dublin City
Clare Nth Tip Offaly Kildare
Limerick South Dublin Dun L Rathd
Lim City Sth Tip Laois Wicklow
Kerry Cork Kilk Crlw Wexford
Cork City Wf Wf City

Ireland 3,917,336; Northern Ireland 1,685,267; Island Total 5,602,603

Arm Armagh, *Banb* Banbridge, *Bmo* Ballymoney, *Bma* Ballymena, *Cfg* Carrickfergus, *Ckst* Cookstown, *Col* Coleraine, *Crgvn* Craigavon, *Crlw* Carlow, *Cstlrgh* Castlereagh, *Dngn* Dungannon, *Dun L Rathd* Dun Laoghaire Rathdown, *Ferm* Fermanagh, *Kilk* Kilkenny, *Lf* Longford, *Lrn* Larne, *Lt* Leitrim, *Lv* Limavady, *Mft* Magharafelt, *Ml* Moyle, *Mon* Monaghan, *N Dn* North Down, *Nwry & M* Newry & Mourne, *Nwtnby* Newtownabbey, *Oma* Omagh, *Rosc* Roscommon, *Strb* Strabane, *Tip* Tipperary, *Wf* Waterford, *Wmth* Westmeath

HEADLINE NEWS

U.S. TO GIVE $50 TO INDONESIA — *Irish Times*

COMMISSION DETERMINED TO HOLD LINE ON FISH TALKS — *Irish Times*

GOVERNMENT MOVES ON STRAY HORSES — *Northside People*

BALLYMUN GARDEN TALKS — *Northside People*

FISH STUDY AGREEMENT — *Irish Independent*

LONGFORD MAN ACTING LIKE A CAVAN MAN — *Anglo Celt*

LYRICS OF THE SASH

It is old but it is beautiful, and its colours they are fine,
It was worn at Derry, Aughrim, Enniskillen and the Boyne.
My father wore it as a youth in bygone days of yore,
And on the Twelfth I love to wear the sash my father wore.

Sure I'm an Ulster Orangeman,
from Erin's isle I came,
To see my British brethren
all of honour and of fame,
And to tell them of my forefathers
who fought in days of yore,
That I might have the right to wear
the sash my father wore.

For those brave men who crossed the
Boyne have not fought or died in vain,
Our Unity, Religion,
Laws and Freedom to maintain.
If the call should come we'll follow
the drum, and cross that river once more,
That tomorrow's Ulsterman may wear
the sash my father wore.

And when some day, across the sea
to Antrim's shore you come,
We'll welcome you in royal style,
to the sound of flute and drum,
And Ulster's hills shall echo still,
from Rathlin to Dromore,
As we sing again the loyal strain
of the sash my father wore.

THOSE WERE THE DAYS

From the Irish Catholic Directory of 1928

"In recent years the dangerous occasions of sin had been multiplied. The old Irish dances had been discarded for foreign importations which, according to all accounts, lent themselves not so much to rhythm as to low sensuality. The actual hours of sleep had been turned into hours of debasing pleasure. Company-keeping under the stars of night had succeeded in too many places to the good old Irish custom of visiting, chatting and story-telling from one house to another, with the Rosary to bring all home in due time. Parental control had been relaxed, and fashions bordering on decency had become a commonplace; while bad books, papers and pictures were finding their way into remote country places."
— *Archbishop Gilmartin*

ISLAND'S LONGEST NEWSPAPER TITLES

Newtownards Chronicle & County Down Observer	Down
Carrickfergus Advertiser & East Antrim Gazette	Antrim
Nationalist & Munster Advertiser	Tipperary
Westmeath & Offaly Independent	Westmeath
Nationalist & Leinster Times	Carlow

Shortest: *Lá* (Belfast); *Foinse* (Galway); *The Echo* (Tallaght).

IRISH RUGBY TACTICS

Against Romania, 1980

"We had decided to go out in the first half and soften them up and kick the proverbial shit out of them." — *Mick Doyle*

"And it went so well that we had a quiet word at half time and decided to kick the shit out of them in the second half." — *Willie Duggan*

FIVE IRISH INDUSTRIES THAT PAY MEN MORE THAN WOMEN

Industrial Sector	*Women*	*Men*	*Bonus*
Electricity, Gas & Water	€ 352	€ 750	+113%
Basic & Fabricated Metal	€ 282	€ 476	+69%
Mining & Quarrying	€ 399	€ 646	+62%
Pulp, Paper & Printing	€ 355	€ 572	+61%
Transport Equipment	€ 363	€ 581	+60%

CSO 2002. Pay levels in 2001.

THE PERCENTAGE GAME

THE LEAGUE OF IRELAND'S MOST CONSISTENT CLUBS

Club	*Years*	*P*	*W*	*D*	*Pts*	*%*
Shamrock Rovers	1922-03	1933	959	456	3333	57
Reds United	1935-36	22	12	1	37	56
Cork United/Athletic	1939-57	316	155	59	524	55
Shelbourne United	1922-24	40	20	6	66	55
Dolphin	1930-37	142	68	25	229	54
Derry City	1987-03	520	224	150	822	53
Cork City	1984-03	567	246	155	893	52
Evergreen United	1951-59	176	81	32	275	52
Fordsons	1924-30	108	51	15	119	52
Bohemians	1922-03	1952	838	459	2973	51
Dundalk	1926-03	1763	763	428	2717	51
Cork Hibernians	1957-76	476	204	120	732	51

Calculated at 3 points for a win; Premier Division record Aug 1922-Mar 2003.

IRISH MUSICAL ANAGRAMS

CHRISTY MOORE	STORMY, HEROIC
EUROVISION SONG CONTEST	*EVENING'S NOTORIOUS COST*
PAUL HEWSON	HALO SEWN UP

"PROTECTING EVIL-DOERS"

CLAUSES FROM THE CATHOLIC CATECHISM

1868: We have a responsibility for the sins committed by others when we cooperate in them, by not disclosing or not hindering them when we have an obligation to do so, or by protecting evil-doers.

2468-9: Truth consists in showing oneself true in deeds and words, and in guarding against duplicity, dissimulation, and hypocrisy. In justice, as a matter of honour, one man owes it to another to manifest the truth.

2483-6: Lying is the most direct offence against the truth. To lie is to speak or act against the truth in order to lead someone into error. Since it violates the virtue of truth, a lie does real violence to another.

2487: Each offence committed against justice and truth entails the duty of reparation, even if its author has been forgiven. This reparation, moral and sometimes material, must be evaluated in terms of the extent of the damage inflicted.

Clause 2487 ends with the reminder that reparation "obliges in conscience".

VOX POP

"I have two teenage children, one is 21 and one is 25."
— Caller to *Gay Byrne Show*

"I went to five (motor insurance) companies in Galway, and both of them refused me." — Caller to Joe Duffy's *Liveline*

"I ran out of the Mater Hospital, screaming and cursing the Lord above. I said: 'There is no God!'"
— Caller to *Today with Pat Kenny*

"If he admitted guilt he must have known that it was non-consensual rape." — Caller to *Gay Byrne Show*

"I'd like to be a pop singer and, if not, I'd like to be a cash register." — Young contributor to *5-7 Live*

CROSSED LINES

Irish Times	*In Dublin*
On 10 June 1993, an epic 105-line poem graced an entire page of the *Irish Times*. It reputedly cost the poet, Sinéad O'Connor, £11,000.	On 26 June 1993, *In Dublin* magazine published the following short poem: *There was a young girl called Sinéad* *To whom not enough attention was paid* *She was basically good* *But misunderstood* *Fuck off! Fuck off! Everybody fuck off!*

THE 'OLD MONEY' IRISH COINS, 1928-1971

Coin	*Value*	*Name*	*Reverse*	*Front*
¼d	Farthing	Feoirling	Woodcock	Harp
½d	Halfpenny	Leath Phingin	Sow & piglets	Harp
1d	Penny	Pingin	Hen & chicks	Harp
3d	Threepence	Leath Reul	Hare	Harp
6d	Sixpence	Reul	Wolfhound	Harp
1s	One shilling	Scilling	Bull	Harp
2s	Two shillings	Flóirín	Salmon	Harp
2s 6d	Two and six	Leath Choróin	Horse	Harp

12d = 1s, 20s = £1. 10s coin minted 1966 to commemorate Easter Rising.

THE MEN BEHIND THE WIRE

Green Version	*Orange Version*
Armoured cars and tanks and guns Came to take away our sons But every man must stand behind The men behind the wire	When the judge had passed my sentence and the warder took me down I cried out No Surrender bless the red hand and the crown But grant me just one favour, that is my one desire Please let me serve my sentence with the men behind the wire

"HE HAS GIVEN US HIS SHOE"

SPIKE MILLIGAN'S CAMEO IN LIFE OF BRIAN

"Stop! Stop! Stop, I say! Stop! Let us… let us pray.
Yea, he cometh to us, like the seed to the grain…"

(Notices that crowd has gone. Shuffles off to side.)

AN ALLITERATIVE SHOPPING LIST

Basic Foods	*Snacks & Sweets*	*Other Products*
Bachelors Beans	Cadbury's Caramel	Archer's Aqua Water
Bar-B-Bar Spices	Coolmine Cakes	Belvedere Bond Paper
Brennan's Bread	Dairylea Dunkers	Born Blonde Hair Dye
Flahavan's Flour	Dorito Dips	Brown Brothers' Wine
Gino Ginelli Pizza	Juicy Jellies	Daily Defense Shampoo
Green Giant Corn	Kit Kat	Fisherman's Friend
Yoplait Yogurt	Tic Tacs	Spick 'n' Span Cloths

THE FIRST 21 YEARS OF THE DUBLIN WOMEN'S MINI-MARATHON

Year	Winner	Time			
1983	Kathy Schilly	34.02	1993	Rosie Lambe	34.25
1984	Regina Joyce	32.34	1994	Mary Donohoe	33.11
1985	Regina Joyce	33.31	1995	Catherine Shum	33.21
1986	Greta Hickey	34.33	1996	Katy McCandless	32.44
1987	Sue Collier	34.02	1997	Catríona McKiernan	32.31
1988	Patricia Griffin	33.57	1998	Catríona McKiernan	33.22
1989	Patricia Griffin	34.28	1999	Catríona McKiernan	33.14
1990	Christine Kennedy	34.17	2000	Sonia O'Sullivan	31.28
1991	Catherine Smith	34.29	2001	Magdaline Chemjor	32.56
1992	Monica Reilly	33.41	2002	Pauline Curley	34.20
			2003	Sonia O'Sullivan	33.21

10 km run-jog-walk. 400,000 women from 15 countries have raised €60m for charity. Annual entries have risen from 9,000 to almost 38,000. Event has been replicated in Liverpool, Oslo, Berlin, Stockholm, Helsinki and Berne.

EKUNDAYO O'BADMUS

Ekundayo Badmus, a Nigerian-born accountant, was the 2000 Irish Monopoly champion. He changed his name by deed poll to O'Badmus for the world championship where he finished 15th.

LONGEST IRISH TOWN NAMES

(SINGLE-WORD AND UNHYPHENATED)

Newtownmountkennedy	19	Bennettsbridge	14
Newtowncunningham	17	Carrickmacross	14
Castlebellingham	16	Courtmacsherry	14
Ballaghaderreen	15	Crocknamurleog	14
Glencolumbkille	15	Edgeworthstown	14
Graiguenamanagh	15	Leighlinbridge	14
Manorcunningham	15	O'Briensbridge	14
Ballyjamesduff	14	Rochfortbridge	14
Ballymulcashel	14	Watergrasshill	14

13: Bailieborough, Ballylongford, Butlersbridge, Carrigtwohill, Castleblayney, Castleconnell, Castlegregory, Castlepollard, Drumcollogher, Portarlington, Portlaoighise, Shannonbridge, Sixmilebridge, Twomileborris.

THE FATHER JACK OIREACHTAS AWARDS

FOR BEST PARLIAMENTARY USE OF FECK, ARSE AND GOBSHITE

David Norris (Ind Senator) in July 1992 on the family planning bill: "Why are we fecking around in this pettifogging way?"

Brendan McGahon (FG TD) in Feb 1997 on the peace process: "What we were offered was a mirage, a phoney peace, which attracted many gobshites."

Emmet Stagg (Labour TD) in June 1988 on the financial estimates: "There was an old saying in my part of the country that there was no need to rub the fat pig's arse in lard. Effectively the Common Agricultural Policy did that."

FOUR REFERENCES TO EVIL IN OIREACHTAS LAW

District Court Rules 1997 excludes from industrial school children who "exercise an evil influence on other children".

Royal Charter of Physicians Amendment Act 1979 deletes a reference to "abuses, evils and mischiefs" of physicians.

Housing Act 1966 refers to "defects and evils" discovered in rented houses that are dangerously overcrowded.

Dispensary Rules 1923 oblige medical officers to "prevent or mitigate the evil" of infectious diseases in their district.

THE STILLBIRTH OF DEMOCRACY IN NORTHERN IRELAND

1920: Local Govt elections held throughout Ireland using Proportional Representation.

1921: Partition comes into effect. NI Nationalist councils say state is illegitimate.

1922: PR is abolished in NI; boundaries redrawn. 13 of 24 Nationalist majorities vanish.

1929: PR now abolished for electing MPs. Unionists win by landslide. Nationalists despair.

1933: Unionists win General Election before a vote is cast. 27 of 52 seats uncontested.

1965: Safe seat is contested: South Antrim voters go to polls for 1st time since 1929.

(In 1958, future NI Prime Minister Captain Terence O'Neill floated the idea of draining Lough Neagh to create a seventh County of Northern Ireland.)

FEMALE-DOMINATED BELIEF SYSTEMS

Belief	*Adherents*	*Women*	*%*
Lutheran	3,068	1,904	62.1
Evangelical	3,780	2,059	54.5
Jehovah's Witness	4,430	2,399	54.2

Census 2002. Methodists are 50:50 women and men.

POWER TO THE PEOPLE

In 2002 Ireland's Cllrs were paid €25m in allowances and expenses. FF's Jimmy Maloney of Mayo got €75,000. Labour's Paula Desmond of Cork got €74,600. 230 got over €40,000 each. From Nov 1998 to April 1999, four Carlow Cllrs got expenses of £2,331 each for attending a single one-hour Strategic Policy Committee meeting. A staff union dispute had stopped other meetings from going ahead.

RESIGNING MATTERS

SEVEN FIANNA FÁIL TDS WHO RESIGNED DESPITE NOT BEING ASKED TO DO SO BY BERTIE AHERN

Michael Collins resigned from FF Parliamentary Party in Sep 2003. Settled tax evasion bill of €130,000, reported the week his colleague GV Wright TD drunkenly drove into a nurse.

Ned O'Keefe, Junior Minister, resigned in Dec 2001. Voted against feeding of bonemeal to animals, forgetting to inform Dáil his family was involved in manufacturing the substance.

Beverly Cooper-Flynn resigned from Public Accounts Comm in Apr 2001. Lost libel case after RTE reported she sold banking products to help tax evaders. Faced £2m legal bill.

Liam Lawlor resigned from FF Parliamentary Party in June 2000, and later as vice-chairman of Oireachtas Ethics Comm. Later jailed for failing to co-operate with Flood Tribunal.

Denis Foley resigned from FF Parliamentary Party in Feb 2000. Had £100,000 in illegal offshore account. Was "hoping against hope" his account was not an Ansbacher one.

John Ellis resigned as chair of Agriculture Comm in Nov 1999. Owed farmers money, had £250,000 written off by NIB, and CJ Haughey gave him £26,000 of taxpayers' cash.

Ray Burke resigned as Govt Minister and TD in Oct 1997. Flood Tribunal later found he had corruptly received almost £200,000, including acquisition of house in Swords.

'BLOCK A REVENUE AUDIT'

1991: Revenue PR campaign (Dodgers Named and Fined: Pay Your Tax or Pay the Penalty), then 128 'little' people named and shamed, including priests, grocers and drapers.	*1992:* Revenue issues its inspectors with the handbook 'Block a Revenue Audit' and tells them to pass it onto big business, instructing how to block out the same inspectors.

PLACES TO FIND TYPES OF PEOPLE

Placename	*From Gaelic*	*Meaning*
Athenry	Átha an Rí	Ford of the kings
Ballintaggart	Baile an tSagairt	Home of the priest
Ballyneanor	Baile an Aonfhir	Home of the lone man
Inchigeelagh	Inse Geimleach	Island of the prisoner
Kilmoyley	Cill Mhaoile	Church of the bald person
Knockcroghery	Cnoc an Chroicaire	Hill of the hangman
Lisnagarvey	Lios na gCearrbach	Fort of the gamblers
Meenaneary	Mín an Aoire	Smooth place of the satirist
Monea	Má Niadh	Plain of the champion
Rathnamuddagh	Ráth na mBodach	Fort of the clowns

1 Galway; 2 Armagh, Down, Kerry; 3 Tyrone; 4 Cork; 5 Kerry; 6 Roscommon; 7 Down; 8 Donegal; 9 Fermanagh; 10 Westmeath.

THE LONG & SHORT OF IT

Contract provisions for temporary Standing Solicitor employed by Clare Co Council, 1976.

"1. The engagement is part-time, temporary, and is not an office or employment of the Council."

"9. The engagement shall terminate on your reaching the age of 65 years. It may, however, be extended."

COST OF TAOISEACH'S MAKE-UP

Year	*Monthly*	*Weekly*	*Year*	*Monthly*	*Weekly*
1998	€ 2034	€ 465	2001	€ 1467	€ 338
1999	€ 1435	€ 331	2002	€ 1537	€ 355
2000	€ 1786	€ 412	2003	€ 2174	€483

Total cost to taxpayer May 98-Mar 03: € 40,000. Total cost to taxpayer of Tánaiste's make-up during same period: € 0.00

STAR SIGNS OF IRELAND'S NOBEL PRIZE WINNERS

Aquarius	Mairead Corrigan 1976, Seán MacBride 1974
Aries	Samuel Beckett 1969, Seamus Heaney 1995
Gemini	Betty Williams 1976, William Butler Yeats 1923
Libra	David Trimble 1998, Ernest Walton 1951
Capricorn; Leo	John Hume 1998; George Bernard Shaw 1925

Peace: Corrigan, Hume, MacBride, Trimble, Williams. Literature: Beckett, Heaney, Shaw, Yeats. Physics: Walton.

THE ORANGE MARCHING SEASON

Easter Mon	App Boys	Sat Pre-12th	Scottish OO
Easter Tue	Junior OO	Sun Pre-12th	Boyne
Mid May	Scot App Boys	12th July	No Surrender!
End of May	Junior OO	13th July	Royal Black
1st Fri June	Mini-12th	Start Aug	District Black
1st Sat June	App Boys	Sat Nearest 12th	App Boys
June Weekends	Mini-12ths	During Aug	Local Black
1st Sun July	Somme	Last Sat Aug	County Black
1st Wed July	Mini-12th	September	More Parades
Sat Pre-12th	Donegal OO	Last Sat Sep	End of Season

Key dates only; hundreds of small parades and commemorations take place all year round. App Boys: Apprentice Boys. OO: Orange Order. Black: Royal Black Institution. Source: CAIN Conflict Archive, Ulster University.

INDEX-LINKED MORALITY

1940s Q: May Catholics vote for any non-Christian (i.e. Jewish) candidates?

A: It is not desirable, but not unlawful, providing the Jew agrees to act in accordance with Christian principles.

1960s Q: To get a job in a Protestant factory, may a Catholic claim to have gone to a non-Catholic school?

A: If the school took only non-Catholic pupils, this amounts to an implicit denial of the True Faith, and is gravely wrong. *(However, as the interview board is bigoted, it may be deceived with an evasive answer that conceals your faith.)*

1960s Q: May a priest urge boycotting non-Catholic traders?

A: Yes, assuming the boycott is for a morally good purpose. Catholics who combine in this way do not infringe any right of non-Catholic merchants.

1960s Q: How much do you have to steal to make the matter a grave (e.g. a mortal rather than a venial) sin?

A: The question is complicated by the rising cost of living: in 1877 £1 was regarded as grave; by 1914 that standard had risen to £2, which would lead to the conclusion that for a working man, the absolute level now is probably about £8 or £9, or one week's wages.

Abbreviated from answers to questions in 'The Irish Ecclesiastical Record'.

WORDS THAT APPEAR MOST OFTEN IN NAMES OF IRISH PUBS IN EUROPE

Word	*Per '000*	*Word*	*Per '000*	*Word*	*Per '000*
Irish	378	Finnegan	18	Kate/Kitty	11
Murphy	37	Celtic	17	O'Reilly	11
Dubliner	36	Fiddler	17	Shannon	11
Paddy	34	Green	17	Dublin	10
Shamrock	34	Harp	17	Ireland	10
Old/Auld	23	O'Brien	17	James	10
Molly	22	Mulligan	14	Limerick	10
Malone	19	Kelly	12	Nelly	10

From list of 1,000+ Irish pubs in mainland Europe on *EuropeanIrish.com.*

IRISH-BORN SOLDIERS AT THE ALAMO

Samuel Burns	Joseph Hawkins	Jackson Rusk
Andrew Duvalt	James McGee	Burke Trammel
Robert Evans	Robert McKinney	William Ward

(Robert Evans was the last soldier to die at the Alamo.)

THE GOSPELS OF SAIPAN

GOSPEL OF QUINN

Mick produces the *Irish Times* article... Suddenly it's gunfight at the OK Corral, but Mick has no gun... Roy goes off, rat-a-tat-a-tat… It is the most articulate, the most surgical slaughtering I have ever heard… Every grievance is ordered and filed neatly with an appropriate insult attached… (The reference to Iran) is Mick belatedly reaching for a weapon, any weapon…

GOSPEL OF MCCARTHY

On Himself: Roy explodes... I struggle to get a word in edgeways… I ask him why he pulled out of the trip to Iran just hours after telling me he was going.

On Keane: For about eight minutes I am every expletive imaginable from c to w. I was a crap player. I am a crap manager. I am a crap coach… I have never seen a human being act like this before. He is delirious… He tells me to stick the World Cup up my fucking arse. Then he is up and gone.

GOSPEL OF KEANE

On McCarthy: "You've gone against your team-mates… You never wanted to play for your country. You were supposed to go to Iran and you didn't, you faked an injury to get out of playing for your country."

On Himself: "You know that's not true… You're a fucking wanker. I didn't rate you as a player, I don't rate you as a manager, and I don't rate you as a person. You're a fucking wanker and you can stick your World Cup up your arse. I've got no respect for you."

PROPOSED IRISH FEAST DAYS

28 Feb: Father Ted Day. In 1998 Dermot Morgan died on the 54th anniversary of men and women being allowed to sit together at the Clones cinema.	*31 July: Not the Full Penny Day.* In 1985 thousands saw a moving statue in Ballinspittle on the 16th anniversary of the withdrawal of the ha'penny.

FIRST OFFICIAL RULES OF THE GAA, 1884

Teams: Not less than 14 or more than 21 players a side.

Scoring: Soccer-style goals, no points. Most goals wins.

Goal size: 15 ft x 8 ft for football; 20 x 10 for hurling.

Start: Before the ball is thrown up, the players from each team stand in two ranks opposite each other, each man holding the hand of one of the other side. Hurlers may either hold hands or cross hurleys.

Uniform: Knee-breeches and stockings and boots or shoes.

Duration: 1 hour for football; 1 hour 20 minutes for hurling.

Pitch: 120 yds x 80 yds for football; 200 x 150 for hurling.

Forbidden: Pushing, tripping, holding from behind; butting with the head; striking with hurleys; boots with protruding nails or iron-tips. Wrestling and 'handigrips' were forbidden in 1886; 'vicious play' in 1888.

Adopted in December 1884 at the second convention of the Gaelic Athletic Association for the Preservation and Cultivation of National Pastimes. In 1886 it was recommended that all dress material etc. be of Irish manufacture.

SIX IRISH COUNTIES THAT ARE ALLOWABLE SCRABBLE WORDS

1	Cork	3	Down	5	Limerick
2	Derry	4	Kerry	6	Mayo

(Official Scrabble Words, International Edition.)

LONGEST HYPHENATED IRISH TOWN NAMES

Laytown-Bettystown-Mornington	Aghada-Farsid-Rostellan
Graiguenamanagh-Tinnahinch	Dún Laoghaire-Rathdown
O'Briensbridge-Montpelier	Bunclody-Carrickduff
Castlebellingham-Kilsaran	Ballybofey-Stranorlar
Lanesborough-Ballyleague	Castlecomer-Donaguile

TEN UNSUNG IRISH CREATORS

Robert Barker	Artist	The first 360° panorama painting
Louis Brennan	Inventor	Invented the first guided missile
James Daly	Promotor	Invented the word 'quiz' for a bet
Cedric Gibbons	Art Director	Designed the Oscar statuette
James Hoban	Architect	Designed the White House
John Holland	Engineer	Invented the modern submarine
Sean Mulhall	Dentist	Christopher Lee's Dracula fangs
Adee Phelan *	Hairdresser	David Beckham's Mohican
Francis Rynd	Doctor	Invented the hypodermic syringe
Denis Santry	Architect	Designed Singapore Golden Dome

* Adee Phelan presented The Salon on Channel 4 in 2003

FASTEST GROWING IRISH RELIGIOUS BELIEFS

Belief	*% 1991*	*% 2002*	*% Change*
No Religion	1.92	3.60	+ 1.68
Church of Ireland	2.59	3.01	+ 0.42
Muslim (Islamic)	0.11	0.49	+ 0.39
Orthodox	0.01	0.27	+ 0.26
Presbyterian	0.38	0.54	+ 0.15

Census 1991-2002. None of these is remotely near Roman Catholicism, which — despite dropping by 3.6% — still commands the nominal allegiance of 90.2% of Irish people.

CRAGGY ISLAND'S FUNLAND

Chair of Death	*Hen Chariots*	Tarot Reading
Duck Startling	The Ladder *	*Tunnel of Goats*
Freak Pointing	*O'Leary's Sweets*	Whirly-go-Round
Goading the Fierce Man	Pond of Terror	*Spider Baby (not real)*
	Spinning Cat	

* Safety warning: "Keep your hands on the sides!"

WHO OWNS ROCKALL?

Rockall is 20m high, 25m wide and 30m long. The UK claims sovereignty over the 'island'. Ireland, Norway and Denmark insist it is an uninhabitable rock, over which nobody can claim sovereignty.

1955, UK. A British Navy helicopter expedition plants a Union Flag; cements a bronze plaque claiming possession.

1955, J Abrach Mackay. The chief of the Scottish Mackay clan formally demands that the Admiralty get off his property.

1972, UK. Her Majesty the Queen stamps the Rockall Act, formally annexing the 'island', not 'rock', for the Crown.

1974, UK. London declares a 50-mile exclusion zone and lands two guards and a sentry box for a photo opportunity.

1980s, UK. John Ridgeway and Tom Mclean each spend a period living there in a bid to give it valid island status.

1997, Waveland. Greenpeace activists set a new endurance record of 42 days and claim the rock for Waveland.

TEN DUBLIN PRONUNCIATIONS

Arthuritis	the disease	*Europes*	the new currency
Axe	to query something	*Goldiekeeper*	at football match
Deffiny	without doubt	*Motrified*	very embarrassed
Erdle Stree	Earl Street	*Skarla*	quite embarrassed
Edgemacation	learning	*Thrun*	past tense of throw

THE BEATLES' IRISH GRANDPARENTS

John Lennon

Father's father, James Lennon, was born in Dublin.
Father's mother, Mary Polly Maguire, was Irish.

Paul McCartney

Father's father, James McCartney, was born in Ireland.
Mother's father, Owen Mohin, was born in Monaghan.

George Harrison

Mother's father, John French, was born in Wexford.

CRUSADING IRISH ANAGRAMS

EAMON DUNPHY	ANNOYED HUMP
GENE KERRIGAN	*REEKING ANGER*
KEVIN MYERS	VERMIN KEYS

THE RED FLAG FLAGS

Mary Robinson, as the first Labour-nominated President, sacked eight elderly staff two weeks before Christmas 1990. She had found twenty-nine dead bluebottles on a window sill and too much cutlery on her table, and she "didn't like the housekeeper".

Ruairí Quinn, Labour Finance Minister, was preparing his 1996 budget when a letter invited businesspeople to pay £100 for "a rare opportunity to gain access to the Minister". Eithne Fitzgerald TD, author of the Ethics in Public Office Act, authored the dinner invite.

Emmet Stagg, Labour junior Minister in 1992, immediately gave state jobs to his daughter and his cousin. Responding to accusations of ethically unsound behaviour, he insisted that: "If it had been nepotism, I would have employed my wife's cousin as well."

PATENTS GRANTED IN IRELAND, 2003

A chair or the like with facilitated assembly	1042976
An interactive television broadcast system	1052854
A perfusion system for organs or body parts	1062870
An automatic vending machine with new cooling system	1076213
Applying a flowable material onto a flat substrate	1093859
An improved rake	1100304
A suction conveyor belt	1110882
A lamp	1122488
A device to record pictures of parcel surfaces	1124651
A method for sanitizing food products	1132012
A shoe insert	1139808
A push button	1151451
A self-inking hand stamp	1152899
A heatable steering wheel	1156956
A device for filling bottles and cans with liquid	1162167
A flying shear	1171258
A break-out device	1181604
A rotating extruder nozzle structure	1183143
A highly-flexible elastic hinge	1194808

PLANES, TRAINS AND AUTOMOBILES

"The four-seater Cessna plane crashed in a rainstorm killing the little girl and her two passengers. It also shattered her dream to enter the Guinness Book of Records."

The Examiner

"I too was amazed to find a condom vending machine in Connolly Station, particularly in view of Iarnrod Éireann's well-earned reputation of always pulling out in time."

Irish Independent

"Cllr Seán Óg Kane raised the issue of hand rails which have been damaged or removed, and wondered what would happen if a child falls in front of a lorry."

Donegal Democrat

CHILDREN'S GAMES PRE-PLAYSTATION

Ball Games	Headies, Kerbs	Queeny-io
Bicycle Races	Hide & Seek	Relievio
Card Games	Hop Scotch	Risk, Campaign
Catapults	Keepy Uppy	Scrabble
Chasing, Running	Kick the Can	Skipping
Chess	Knick Knocks	Slaps
Climbing Trees	London Bridge	Subbuteo
Cluedo, Colditz	Looby Light	Swimming
Conkers	Marbles	Swings
Doctors & Nurses	Mastermind	Table Tennis
Draughts	Monopoly	Tennis
Falling Soldiers	Mulberry Bush	Big Ship Sails
Football Tennis	Poles	Three & In
Giant Steps	Postman's Knock	Tunnel of Thumps

THOSE WERE THE DAYS

"Wooden roadside platforms were set on fire by curates; surer still, the priests drove motor cars back and forward over the timber platforms; concertinas were set flying into hill streams, and those who played music were branded as outcasts." — Kerry playwright *Bryan McMahon* recalls the '20s and '30s

MAINLAND EUROPEAN CITIES WITH MOST IRISH PUBS

Paris	France	50	Amsterdam	Holland	11
Berlin	Germany	45	Brussels	Belgium	11
Vienna	Austria	22	Prague	Czech Rep	11
Rome	Italy	14	Frankfurt	Germany	10
Hamburg	Germany	13	Munich	Germany	10

From list of 1,000+ Irish pubs in mainland Europe on *EuropeanIrish.com.*

AN IRISH BLIND DATE

Green	Favourite Colour	Orange
Lily	Favourite Flower	Poppy
1916	Most Memorable Date	1690
Not an Ounce	Most Likely To Say	Not an Inch
Palestinians	Favourite Other Nation	Israelis
Protesting	Favourite Activity	Marching
Marchers	Most Irritated By	Protesters
Occupied 6 Counties	Address	United Kingdom

UNCONTROVERSIAL RESEARCH FINDINGS FROM UCC

Diet. We should eat more fruit and vegetables. Evidence shows dietary factors may lie behind the rise in mortality from heart disease and certain cancers over the last century.

Obesity. Fast food and junk food is increasingly marketed to children. Unless tackled, this will cause major problems in future years, both with obesity and economically.

Corruption. Is to be found where politicians have a direct role in specific decisions of high value to wealthy business interests, and where civil servants have lax accountability systems.

Play. Parents should actively play with their children if they want to be influential in their life. Play should be enjoyable and freely chosen, with no outside 'learning' goals.

Diet: Dr Nora O'Brien, 2002; Obesity: Prof Ivan Perry, 2001; Corruption: Prof Neil Collins, 2001; Play: Dr Marian Murphy, 2001.

THE EMBRACE OF LOVE

In 1941 Kate O'Brien's novel, *The Land Of Spices*, was banned because it contained the sentence: "She saw Etienne and her father, in the embrace of love." (Etienne was a man.)

IRISH WOMEN OF INFLUENCE

Catherine McCauley. Opened House of Mercy orphanage in 1800s. Later became a nun and founded Sisters of Mercy.

Ninette de Valois. Founder of Royal Ballet in 1935. Dame of British Empire. Taught Rudolf Nureyev.

Eileen Gray. A Paris-based early 20th Century pioneer of modern furniture, interior design and architecture.

Mairín de Burca and Mary Anderson. In a 1975 court case, overturned the exclusion of women from Irish juries.

THE PARNELL NATIONAL TRIBUTE, 1884

USA	£5,745	Kildare	£867	Monaghan	£469
Cork	2,860	Kerry	830	Roscommon	431
Tipperary	2,828	Wicklow	796	Down	372
Limerick	2,620	Louth	695	Donegal	370
Australia	2,222	Queen's Co	693	Longford	352
Dublin	1,919	Carlow	666	Canada	340
Wexford	1,918	Galway	658	Leitrim	291
Clare	1,563	Cavan	656	Antrim	290
Kilkenny	1,455	King's Co	537	Sligo	243
England	1,440	Buenos Aires	506	Fermanagh	233
Meath	1,343	Scotland	489	Armagh	232
Waterford	1,144	Tyrone	487	Derry	209
Westmeath	869	Misc	478	Mayo	173

When Charles Stewart Parnell faced the loss of his estate, ordinary people collected almost £40,000 to help him. The collection gathered pace after it was condemned by the Pope. Queen's Co, King's Co now Laois, Offaly.

CLASSIC *EVENING HERALD* TYPO

"(The 1951 Census is) the biggest census of copulation ever undertaken by the State."

HEADLINES FROM THE FIRST *EVENING PRESS*, 1954

Jails in Ireland are Doing Less Business
"Crime figures plummet as criminals realise 'crime doesn't pay'."

Boy Will Play Uileann Pipes Hitler Wanted
"Fuehrer was so interested he called Goering and Goebbels over."

Bachelors Use Clubs Against Women
"Rule Number One is 'Each member must be a bachelor'."

Flying Saucers Over England?
"Rye estate agent said they appeared to travel at 2,000 mph."

Issue 2 front page headline:
Evening Press an Immediate Success

THE CANON LAW PENALTY FOR PAEDOPHILIA

Canon Law? Code of internal rules of Catholic Church. Law 1395.2 covers sexual offences, including with a minor.

1917 Code: Offenders "shall be suspended, declared infamous, deprived of every office, benefice, dignity or position that they may hold, and in more grievous cases they shall be deposed".

1983 Code: Pope John Paul II introduces new code of Canon Law: A paedophile is now "to be punished with just penalties, not excluding dismissal from the clerical state if the case so warrants".

2001 Update: Bishops now no longer free to deal with such cases. May only conduct a preliminary investigation, then contact Vatican. Lay persons precluded from involvement.

Cases are now subject to the 'Pontifical Secret'. Details to be sent directly to Vatican, not (as before) kept in secret Diocesan archives for ten years and then destroyed.

Vatican sets up two tribunals to handle new workload. Does not publish norms under which these tribunals will work. Says it will send them to Bishops on an 'as needed' basis.

BEYOND THE PALE

Twelve insensitive Dublin terms for country-dwellers

Benjy Riordan	Bogger	Mulchie
Bog monster	Culchie	Mullah
Bog slasher	Muck savage	Redneck
Bog trotter	Mucker	Slurry muncher

One insensitive country term for Dublin-dwellers

Jackeen = Small waver of the Union Jack

I HAVE BIDDEN FAREWELL…

Dr Noel Browne, as Health Minister in the 1948-51 Inter-Party Government, proposed a healthcare scheme known as the Mother & Child service. Catholic medics and Bishops opposed it. Browne stood firm. His party leader Seán MacBride demanded that he resign. Some extracts from Browne's reply… (11 Apr 1951) .

Dear Mr MacBride: "I received your letter (which) is a model of the two-faced hypocrisy and humbug so characteristic of you. Your reference to a conflict between the spiritual and temporal authorities will occasion a smile among the many people who remember the earlier version of your kaleidoscopic self…

"On the other side is your envenomed attack on me at the executive committee meeting last Sunday (because) I allowed myself to be photographed with the Protestant Archbishop of Dublin. This puerile bigotry is scarcely calculated to assist the cause of national reunification which you profess to have at heart…

"I have tried to analyse your curious philosophy, but not very successfully. Expediency is your sole yardstick, and to expediency you are prepared to subordinate all principles sacred and profane. I have bidden farewell to your unwholesome brand of politics… I am today sending my letter of resignation …"

THE FIRST RECORDED HURLING MATCH

Teams: Fir Bolg (home) v Tuatha De Danann. *Venue:* Moytura, near Cong, County Mayo. *Date:* 1272 BC, given in The Book of Leinster. *Rules:* 27-man teams. No quarter asked or given.	*Match Report:* "They played until their bones were broken and bruised and they fell outstretched on the earth. Then the victors fell upon their opponents and slew them." *Winners:* Fir Bolg won the match. *However:* Tuatha De Danann won the ensuing battle, and Ireland.

HOSPITABLE IRISH PLACENAMES

Placename	*From Gaelic*	*Meaning*
Ardavaga	Árd a' Mhagaidh	Height of merriment
Clonmel	Cluain Meala	Pasture of honey
Garynafela	Garraí Na Féile	Garden of the hospitality
Gill Lough	Loch Gile	Lake of brightness
Greenaun	Grianán	Sunny or important place
Iniskeen	Inis Caoin	Beautiful island
Knockanevin	Cnogán Aoibhinn	Pleasant small hill
Phoenix Park	Fionn Uisce	Park of the clear water
Teernacreeve	Tír Dá Craebh	Place of two sacred trees
Toberbunny	Tábair Bainne	Well of milk

1 Offaly; 2 Tipperary, Tyrone; 3 Westmeath; 4 Kilkenny, Limerick, Sligo; 5 Clare, Limerick, Donegal; 6 Louth; 7 Cork; 8 Dublin; 9 Westmeath; 10 Dublin.

DUNPHY ON GAYBO

Early '90s	*1997*	*2003*
"Gone, sad, pathetic."	"I love Mr Gay Byrne… one of the great people in this country."	"A grumpy old man."

Gaybo on Dunphy (2003): "Horrible little crud."

CHURCH & STATE, 1923-1970

16 LAWS AND ONE CONSTITUTION ON WHICH CATHOLIC BISHOPS WERE CONSULTED OR MADE REPRESENTATIONS

Censorship of Films Act	1923
Censorship of Publications Act	1929
Legitimacy Act (Children)	1930
Vocational Education Act	1930
The Constitution of Ireland	1937
Public Health Bill	1945
Health Acts	1947, 53
Intoxicating Liquor (Amendment) Bill	1948
Adoption Acts	1952, 64
Registration of Births, Marriages & Deaths Act	1952
Intoxicating Liquor Act	1960
Agriculture (An Foras Talúntais) Act	1958
Charities Act	1961
Succession Act	1965

Source: *Church & State In Modern Ireland 1923-1970*, JH Whyte.

CAPITAL/FM104 — PANIC STATION

LAUNCH DAY SEQUENCE, 20 JULY 1989

7am	Minister Ray Burke presides at champagne media breakfast.
8am	Phil Lynott's 'Old Town' gets Ireland's 1st independent on air.
8.40	1st news bulletin leads with allegations of a bribes scandal.
9-ish	*Burke enters studio. Breezily slams bribery allegations story.
1pm	**RTE News: Burke insists Capital air 20% news from Day 1.
1.15	RTE News: Capital say granted 1 month derogation by IRTC.
1pm	Burke had already said IRTC had no authority to grant such.
2-ish	Capital brainstorming. Fear legal gag by failed licence rivals.
10pm	First 'current affairs' show airs, a phone-in on topic of radio.

* Burke told producer: "The first morning, the first news bulletin and what do we get? A quote from the Workers' Party!"

** Pre-recorded item. Licence stipulated 20% news or current affairs (4.8 hours daily).

OPENING LINES OF IRISH BOOKS

The kitchen was full of the smells of baking. *Circle Of Friends, Maeve Binchy.*

"We'll ask Jimmy," said Outspan. "Jimmy'll know." *The Commitments, Roddy Doyle.*

Stately, plump Buck Mulligan came from the stairhead, bearing a bowl of lather on which a mirror and a razor lay crossed. *Ulysses, James Joyce.*

Like all government buildings, the interior of the public waiting room in the Department of Social Welfare was drab and uninviting. *The Mammy, Brendan O'Carroll.*

I wakened quickly and sat up in bed abruptly. *The Country Girls, Edna O'Brien.*

"Say what you said, because I know." *The Dark, John McGahern.*

Mrs Brennan took her seat again at the sewing machine by the window. *The Valley Of The Squinting Windows, Brinsley MacNamara.*

VOTE FIANNA FÁIL

"There's always one Ard Fheis that's much better than the others. The Fianna Fail Ard Fheis always brings in lots of business. The Fine Gaelers don't spend money." — *Prostitute Linda Lavelle*

"There are men and women in this country who are alive, who would have been killed in six months' time."
— *Ray Burke TD*

"(U2) were his heroes, though he couldn't stand their music."
— *Niall Andrews* on his dad

"I knock on doors. I listen to people who will not answer because they are frightened."
— *Sen Marian McGuinness*

"A child-minder is self-employed, works in her own home and marries a small number of children."
— *Mary Wallace TD*

"(The Ard Fheis is) my retreat into fantasy."
— *Brian Cowen TD*

"The real test for a dogfood salesman is will he eat his own product for his customers."
— *Albert Reynolds TD*

5-7 LIVE

"Darren Clarke has been partnered with Sergio Garcia, Lee Janzen and himself."
— *Con Murphy*

"And that was Brendan Howlin, the Labour Party Justice spokesman, speaking to me a little later on."
— *Ryan Tubridy*

BEST FIRST-LETTER-OF-SURNAME

IF YOU ARE PLANNING TO RUN FOR THE DÁIL

Ltr	*TDs*	*%*	*Ltr*	*TDs*	*%*	*Ltr*	*TDs*	*%*
M	143	12.8	K	54	4.8	E	16	1.4
C	141	12.6	G	43	3.9	P	16	1.4
B	130	11.6	S	40	3.6	J	8	0.7
O	114	10.2	R	37	3.3	Q	3	0.3
D	78	7.0	W	27	2.4	U	2	0.2
H	71	6.4	A	23	2.1	V	2	0.2
F	70	6.3	T	23	2.1	Y	1	0.1
L	57	5.1	N	17	1.5	I, X, Z	0	0.0

Ltr = first letter of surname; *TDs* = no of TDs elected since 1922 with that first letter; *%* = % of all 1,116 TDs elected since 1922. Each TD is counted only once, so 're-election advantage' does not distort these figures.

MAIN PATTERNS

Over half of all TDs' names start with A to H, and another quarter with M or O (reflecting Irish 'Mac' and 'O' surnames; and most of *these* TDs have an A to H as their next letter).

CANDIDATES' NAMES

In 2002, 28% of new candidates had 'M' or 'O' surnames; this translated to 28% of new TDs. But with 'A' to 'H' names, less than 40% of new candidates translated to 55% of new TDs.

The eight 'QUVY's elected to the Dáil since 1922 are Daniel Vaughan 1922, Timothy Quill 1927, James Victory 1927, Ruairí Quinn 1977, Ivan Yates 1981, Máirín Quill 1987, Pat Upton 1992 and Mary Upton 1997.

TEN U2 NON-STADIUM GIGS

Howth Community Centre	Band's first gig as U2, Mar 1978
Project Arts Centre	Paul McGuinness attends, May 1978
McGonagles, Dublin	Billed below Modern Heirs, July 1978
Liberty Hall, Dublin	Contraceptives rally, Summer 1978
Top Hat, Dun Laoghaire	Support to Stranglers, Sept 1978
Arcadia, Cork	Last on, crowd gone home, Oct 1978
Village Inn, Kilkenny	'Tour de France' of Ireland, Feb 1980
Blue Lagoon, Sligo	Play 'Twilight', 'Cartoon World', Feb 1980
Country Club, Cork	"Riveting", says *NME*, Feb 1980
Bridge House, Tullamore	Tony Stevens tops bill, Feb 1980

WHERE TO HEAR A CÚPLA FOCAIL TODAY

Most			*Least*
Galway County	16.6 %	Dublin City	5.2 %
Donegal	13.0 %	Louth	7.1 %
Kerry	11.1 %	Waterford City	7.2 %
Waterford	10.3 %	Dun Laoghaire	7.4 %
North Tipperary	10.2 %	South Dublin	7.5 %

Census 2002. Daily Irish speakers as percentage of population.

PEOPLE GRANTED HONORARY IRISH CITIZENSHIP

Who	*What*
Chester Beatty	American mining magnate
Tiede & Mrs Herrema	Dutch industrialist & wife
'Tip' & Mildred O'Neill	US Congressman & wife
Alfred & Clementine Beit	English art collector & wife
Jack & Pat Charlton	English footballer & wife
Jean Kennedy Smith	US Ambassador to Ireland
Derek Hill	English painter and collector

ALEX STEVENSON: IRISH RANGER

The only Irish international to play for Glasgow Rangers.
Played for Ireland seven times between 1932 and 1949.
Played for Dolphin, Glasgow Rangers, Everton, St Pat's Athletic.
Scored 90 goals in 270 games for Rangers.
Also won 17 caps for Northern Ireland.

IRISH TELEVISION'S FIRST SATURDAY EVENING SCHEDULE, 6 JAN 1962

5.00 *Tales of Wonder*
Emlyn Williams reads 'A Child's Christmas' by Dylan Thomas.

5.10 *Rin Tin Tin*

5.40 *Children's Corner*
Audrey Meredith 'keeps' the corner for children of all ages. Today, the Cora Cadwell school of dancers.

6.00 *The Angelus*

6.01 *News & Weather*

6.11 *Visitors' Book*
Barry Baker interviews interesting people passing through Ireland this week.

6.45 *The Silent Service*
Bergall's Dilemma: first in a series by Rear Admiral Thomas Dykes about life in the submarine service.

7.15: *For Moderns*
TP McKenna introduces a show for moderns of all ages, but particularly those under 25. Includes the week's brightest records, trends in younger fashion and younger newsmakers. Tonight's show features the Ian Henry Quintet and playwright Kevin Casey.

8.00 *The Twilight Zone*
Where is Everybody? A play by Rod Selling.

8.30 *Jackpot*
Gay Byrne presents a new general knowledge quiz game based on an idea by Cecil Sheridan.

9.00 *News & Weather*

9.15 *The Heiress*
Starring Michael Shane and Richard Denning.

10.15 *The World This Week*
A half-hour's film report of the news this week.

10.45 *An Fear agus a Scéal*
Prionsias MacAonghasa ag caint le Mairtín Ó Direain.

11.00 *Nocturne*
A thought for the night.

11.05 *Nuacht agus Aimsir*

11.15 *Closedown*

DÉJÀ VU, IL DUCE

CJ Haughey — "It was a very good piece of police work. Slowly, painstakingly putting the whole thing together and eventually finding the right man." The Taoiseach finds Malcolm McArthur guilty prior to trial. Judge rules that Haughey made "a bona fide mistake". Case goes ahead.

Mary Harney — "He should be convicted." The Tánaiste argues that CJ Haughey should be jailed, prior to his trial on charges of obstructing the McCracken Tribunal. His judgement day is indefinitely postponed after High Court finds that Harney's comments would prevent a fair trial.

FOUR *IRISH STAR* SCOOPS

'Hail Mary Full of Grace, Drink Your Pint and Leave This Place'. Meath publican clears pub each night by playing tape of Rosary recital.

'Man Who Conned Lord Mayor Held'. An American astronaut, recently awarded honorary freedom of Dublin by Ben Briscoe, is jailed in the USA for fraud, larceny and impersonating an astronaut.

'U2 Snub Awards'. U2 send deputy to collect their 1989 Rehab National Entertainment Award. "The awards are much bigger than U2," says organiser.

'Wee-Wee on Live Lamppost Got Garda All Lit Up'. Off-duty Garda walking his dog is jolted through leash when dog pees on 'live' lamppost. Garda awarded £3,150 from Dublin Corporation.

THREE SUSPECTED COMMIES

SAYS UNITED STATES EMBASSY, 1970

Broadcaster Charlie Bird	League for a Workers Republic
Broadcaster Sean MacReamoinn	Irish Campaign for Peace
Historian John de Courcy-Ireland	Irish-USSR Society

O'CONNELL'S 'MONSTER MEETINGS', 1843

Date	*Venue*	*Attendance*	*Date*	*Venue*	*Attendance*
19 Mar	Trim	100,000	3 Jul	Donnybrook	200,000
19 Apr	Limerick	120,000	9 Jul	Waterford	500,000
23 Apr	Kells	150,000	16 Jul	Tullamore	150,000
9 May	Mullingar	100,000	20 Jul	Enniscorthy	400,000
19 May	Charleville	200,000	23 Jul	Tuam	200,000
21 May	Cork	500,000	30 Jul	Castlebar	400,000
23 May	Cashel	300,000	6 Aug	Baltinglass	150,000
24 May	Nenagh	500,000	15 Aug	Tara	500,000
28 May	Longford	100,000	10 Sep	Loughrea	150,000
8 Jun	Kilkenny	300,000	17 Sep	Clifden	150,000
11 Jun	Mallow	300,000	24 Sep	Lismore	150,000
15 Jun	Ennis	500,000	1 Oct	Mullaghmast	250,000
22 Jun	Skibbereen	500,000	1843	Total	6,870,000

Daniel O'Connell's campaign for Repeal of the Union with Britain was launched in 1840 and peaked 1843. Population of Ireland approx 8 million.

HOW TO PLAY 'BALL AGAINST THE WALL'

Plainy	Throw ball against wall and catch on rebound
Backy	Stand sideways, throw ball behind back against wall
To Backy	Clap hands behind back before catching ball
Basket	Interlock fingers and catch ball in your palms
Bouncy	Bounce ball off ground onto wall, then catch
Burl Around	Turn completely around before catching ball
Clappy	Clap your hands before catching ball on rebound
Downy	Bounce ball off wall onto ground, then catch it
Hippy	Put your hands on your hips before catching ball
Jelly Bag	Hold wrists together, spread fingers, catch ball
Leggy	Throw ball under raised leg, off ground, onto wall
Pipey	Throw ball straight up in the air and catch it
Stampy	Stamp both feet on ground before catching ball
Tippy	Bend and touch ground before catching ball
Under	Throw ball between both legs, off ground, onto wall
Uppie	Throw ball up to a higher spot on the wall

I WAS SKARLA' !

SIX 'MOST EMBARRASSING MOMENTS'

Ronan Collins Introducing the actor Michael Crawford as Michael York.	*Paul McGuinness* Offering RIP condolences to friend. Friend's mom alive.
Fintan O'Toole Being mistakenly 'recognised' as the singer Leo Sayer.	*Moya O'Doherty* "When is next Mass?" London bobby: "This is Parliament!"
Mairín de Burca Mistakenly smashing windows of German Consulate.*	*Frank McDonald* Slating Jury's Cabaret to man. Man's wife singing on stage.

* Trying to smash windows of the British Embassy.

IRISH RELIGIOUS BELIEFS, 1981 AND 2003

Belief	*'81*	*'03*	*Diff*	*Belief*	*'81*	*'03*	*Diff*
God	95%	87%	-8	Afterlife	76%	56%	-20
Sin	85%	66%	-19	The Devil	57%	39%	-18
Heaven	83%	65%	-18	Hell	54%	37%	-17
A Soul	82%	69%	-13	Reincarnation	26%	22%	-4

Amárach Consulting 1981 & Diageo Ireland Quality of Life Survey 2003.

FIT TO GOVERN?

What? In 1978 Senator Lady Valerie Goulding, urged by Health Min Charles Haughey, drew up a fitness regime for Fianna Fáil TDs and Senators.

Why? "It will enable you to rise to the demands of office and set you apart from your less impressive colleagues on the opposite side of the House."

How? 30 minutes, three times a week, on swimming, cycling or jogging. As a bonus: "Your desire for alcohol will most likely diminish."

Phase 1: Started with a two-mile run in the Phoenix Park. Field led home by Liam Lawlor TD, Bertie Ahern TD and Sen Liam Hyland.

ROY KEANE'S FAVOURITE TOPICS

Most Often	*Mentioned in his*	*Autobiography*	*Less Often*
Alex Ferguson	57	Mick McCarthy	8
Manchester United	55	Alf Inge Haaland	6
Eric Cantona	46	Cathal Dervan	3
Brian Clough	41	Charles Haughey	2
Bryan Robson	39	Liam Brady	2
Jack Charlton	30	Jason McAteer	2
Steve Bruce	28	Zenith Data Systems Cup	2
Irish Team/Premiership	27	The League Cup	1
The World Cup	26	Phoenix Park	1

WHY NOT TO CLAIM TO HAVE MADE 'A QUANTUM LEAP'

Described as 'Quantum Leaps'	*Claim made by*
Self development on a Tony Quinn course	Tony Quinn
The FAI's response to the Genesis Report	The FAI
Govt support for the Arts in Ireland	John O'Donoghue
Education Dept spending from 1977-2002	Noel Dempsey
Restructuring of Dept of Education & Science	Michael Woods

A Quantum Leap is an extremely small change at subatomic particle level. The 'leap' is often smaller than the diameter of the nucleus of an atom, and the nature of the change happens entirely at random.

THE TRAGICALLY HIP

TEN VERY EIGHTIES BAND NAMES

Thee Amazing Colossal Men	Shimpu Zig Zag
The How & Why Insects	Those Nervous Animals
Geoffrey's First Affair	Backwards into Paradise
An Emotional Fish	Too Much for the Whiteman
Dogmatic Element	Ghost of an American Airman

"I HAVE NOT DONE THIS INTENTIONALLY"

FROM JAN 2002 DÁIL SPEECH OF LIAM LAWLOR TD

Responding to demands that he resign after being jailed for failing to cooperate with the Flood Tribunal:

I did not see the purpose of (some questions) and I refused to answer. That was a momentous mistake on my behalf because it was interpreted as non-cooperation…

I thought 'discovery' was a television channel, but I have since learned that it is a wider, more complicated and difficult matter...

I hired a big photocopying machine and spent about a day and a half at Christmas discovering every piece of available paper I could…

*Mr Justice Smith found last week that I had still not complied with his order. I have not done this intentionally.**

* Technically, in the context of the first sentence, Lawlor is saying that he intentionally has not complied with the order.

GUGLIELMO MARCONI — IRISH GENIUS

Born Bologna, to Annie Jameson (Whiskey) of Wexford.	*1874*
Invents secret poitín still in attic of family home.	*1880s*
Moves to Jameson stately home in Montrose (now RTE).	*1896*
Broadcast from Rathmines Town Hall astounds crowd.	*1897*
At Kingstown, sends world's first press report by wireless. *	*1898*
Marries the Hon Beatrice O'Brien of Inchiquin, Co Clare.	*1905*
1st transatlantic wireless service, Clifden to Nova Scotia.	*1907*
Joins Mussolini's Fascist Party. Sets-up Vatican Radio.	*1920s*

* From Kingstown Yacht Regatta to the *Dublin Daily Express*.

TWENTY NAMES OF IRISH PUBS IN MAINLAND EUROPE

Pub	Location	Pub	Location
Bean An Tí	Pisa, I	Pig's Nose	Steenwijk, N
Cobblers	Germering, G	Killiwilly	Leipzig, G
Confession Box	Oldenburg, G	L'Antidote	Lyon, F
Craic & Ceol	Lanzarote	Merry Monk	Vienna, A
Crown & Sword	Vienna, A	Mick's Place	Bonn, G
Die Orange	Bremen, G	Murphy's Law	Various
Fat Pat	Balingen, G	Pogue Mahones	Bolzano, A
The Field	Carpaneto, I	Ryan the Poacher	Barzana, I
The GPO	Berlin, G	Shamrockin'	Algarve, P
Hiccup	Dortmund, G	Thursty Nelly's	K'Sltrn, G

A Austria, F France, G Germany, I Italy, N Netherlands, P Portugal. Full name of Confession Box is Murphy's Confession Box. Outside mainland Europe, Kazakhstan has a Mad Murphy's Irish Pub.

WHERE TO MEET A MUSLIM

Most		*Least*	
Fingal	1.14 %	Tipperary North	0.12 %
South Dublin	1.00 %	Monaghan	0.12 %
Galway City	0.98 %	Leitrim	0.13 %
Dublin City	0.86 %	Waterford County	0.13 %
Waterford City	0.72 %	Galway County	0.18 %

Census 2002.

'JUST A MINUTE' QUIZ

Larry Gogan: Complete the phrase. A little learning is ... ?
Contestant: A lot!

Larry Gogan: Complete the phrase. Wine, women and ... ?
Contestant: Sex!

Larry Gogan: What type of person would wear a tutu?
Contestant: A bishop!

Larry Gogan: What 'S' is a native of Liverpool?
Contestant: Scumbag!

EATING HABITS OF IRISH TEENAGERS

Microwavers	Cook for selves, use microwaves	27%
Modern Munchers	Eat out sensibly, snack a lot	20%
Slimmers	Low fat and overtly healthy food	19%
Health Nuts	Health food, not always low fat	18%
Fast Foodies	Fast food restaurants & takeaways	17%

Youthscape Survey. Irish Institute of Advertising Practitioners, 1999.

GULLIVER'S TELESCOPE?

1726. Jonathan Swift writes *Gulliver's Travels*. In chapter 3, the Laputans "have likewise discovered two lesser stars, or satellites, which revolve about Mars". Swift then describes their attributes: "The former revolves in the space of ten hours, and the latter in twenty-one and a half..."

1877. A century and a half later, in real life, at the Naval Observatory in Washington, US astronomer Asaph Hall discovers the two moons of Mars. Their orbital periods are 7.6 and 30.2 hours, not far off the 10 and 21.5 hours of the Martian satellites in Swift's *Gulliver's Travels*.

LOWEST DIVORCE RATES OF PEOPLE WHOSE MARRIAGE HAS ENDED

Area	*Divorce Rate*	*Ended*	*Divorced*	*Separated*
Limerick City	27.9 %	2,818	787	2,031
Cork City	28.3 %	5,171	1,465	3,706
Louth	30.4 %	4,578	1,391	3,187
South Dublin	31.1 %	10,282	3,200	7,082
Waterford City	32.0 %	2,121	678	1,443

Census 2002. Separated includes deserted. Divorced includes remarried after previous divorce. State average is 36.4%.

PUBLICATIONS OF PETER ROBINSON MP

A War to Be Won
Capital Punishment for Capital Crime
Carson, Man of Action
Give Me Liberty
Hands off the UDR
It's Londonderry
IRA-Sinn Féin
Life at the Interface
Savagery and Suffering
Self Inflicted
The North Answers Back
The Union Under Fire
Their Cry Was 'No Surrender!'
Ulster in Peril
Ulster, the Facts
Ulster, the Prey

DOWN WITH THIS SORT OF THING

BANS AND CONDEMNATIONS OF THE 20TH CENTURY

Rev Magee of Cavan condemns immoral postcards	*1910*
Cork students banned from dancing ragtime or one-step	*1921*
Bishops condemn "abnormal craze" for night dancing	*1925*
Limerick mob seize and burn reels of 'Juno & the Paycock'	*1930*
National Athletic & Cycling Association bans women	*1934*
Thurles schoolboys march against blue-shirted classmates	*1934*
Gaelic League asks Dublin Council to oppose jazz music	*1934*
GAA drops Douglas Hyde as patron for attending soccer	*1939*
Russia vetoes Ireland joining the United Nations	*1947*
Aer Lingus bans air hostesses after seven years' service	*1955*
NI Education Dept bans schoolbook with tricolour picture	*1956*
Bishop of Clonfert condemns woman with no nightie	*1966*
Bishop Moynihan stops Jane Mansfield show in Tralee	*1967*
Catholic Bishops lift ban on their flock attending TCD	*1970*
RTE spikes 'The Spike' after nude model appears in art class	*1978*
Courts ban Boomtown Rats concert at Leopardstown	*1980*
Courts ban 14-year-old rape victim from leaving country	*1992*
Ban on divorce is lifted after second referendum is passed	*1997*
GAA votes to keep ban on RUC members	*1998*
Swiss Sports Court upholds ban on Michelle de Bruin	*1999*

DUBLIN'S NEWSTALK 106

"Radon gas is more likely to kill you with lung cancer than drunk driving, drowning or a fire in the home."
— *George Hook*

"The British leader and US President, George Bush, will hold a press conference."
— *Newsdesk*

"Gardaí have seized a quarter kilo of the drug at a house in Kilmainham. It is thought to have arrived by e-mail."
— *Newsdesk*

"Lord Hunt follows Robin Cunt … Robin *Cook!* … out of the cabinet."
— *David McWilliams*

MOST STABLE IRISH MARRIAGES

Area	*Failure Rate*	*Still Married*	*Divorced*	*Separated*
Cavan	6.7 %	22,016	682	888
Galway County	7.1 %	57,188	1,905	2,415
Monaghan	7.3 %	20,344	524	1,063
Limerick County	7.5 %	46,511	1,321	2,383
Roscommon	7.6 %	21,721	777	993

Census 2002. State average is 9.8%. Separated includes deserted.

BRING THEM HOME

The USA 9: In 1994, nine Govt Ministers had pressing business in USA, 'coinciding' with Ireland's World Cup games.

The Florida 8: In 1996 eight Wicklow Cllrs spent a week in Florida discussing housing issues in Hungary, Malaysia and Singapore.

The San Jose 8: In 1996 three Dublin Cllrs were invited on a twinning trip to San Jose, California. Eight Dublin Cllrs attended.

The Guadeloupe 6: In 1995 six FF MEPs took a 'study-trip' to the Caribbean island which, technically, is part of France and hence the EU.

OFF-THE-BALL INCIDENTS

Football: Lansdowne Rd, Ireland v Denmark, 2001. Peter Madsen of Brondby is booed for 20 minutes by Irish Celtic 'fans' who think he is Peter Lovenkrands of Glasgow Rangers.

Gaelic: Croke Park, Laois v Kildare, 2003. Laois bring corner-back Joe Higgins' twin six-year-old sons onto pitch before game as team mascots. GAA fines Laois County Board €1,400.

INHABITANTS OF LYPTON VILLAGE

Bonovox of O'Connell Street	Seán De Angelo
Gavin Friday	Guggi (Guglielmo Marconi)
The Edge	Dave Id Busarus Scott Watson Bang
Pod	The Great Strongman from Southern California

HOT PRESS LETTER OF THE FORTNIGHT

"In view of the controversy about U2 selling out, may I relate my experiences with the band. After a brilliant gig at the LA Coliseum, myself and some friends waited for U2 in the car park. After about 50 minutes, all four band members arrived and started talking to us. They invited us back to their hotel. We had a delicious four-course meal and went for a swim in the luxury pool. Then Bono noticed I had a slight cough and offered to pay for a heart and lung transplant. My friend mentioned that her mother had an incurable illness, so Larry and Adam stayed up all night working on a new antidote. Luckily it worked and her mother is now a big U2 fan! Then Bono gave us £10,000 each. Then, not to be outdone, The Edge promised to buy every one of us a luxury home in the Caribbean! Surely no other band in the world cares as much about their fans as U2!"

— *Sharon Dulux*, Wide Awake in Mulhuddard (1988)

MONETARY REFORM IN ACTION

Oliver J Flanagan was first elected to the Dáil by cycling around his constituency giving passionate after-Mass speeches on his campaign slogan 'Monetary Reform'. Six months later, a constituent asked him why he had stopped talking about monetary reform. Flanagan explained that he used to earn £5 a week as a carpenter, that he now earned £20 a week as a TD, and "that is monetary reform in action".

HOW SLOW IS DUBLIN TRAFFIC?

MINUTES TAKEN TO TRANSPORT A 5 KG PACKAGE 5 KM

City	*Mins*	*City*	*Mins*	*City*	*Mins*
Singapore	9	Dubai, Tokyo	16	Cairo	29
Johannesburg	12	New York	17	Chennai	35
London	13	San Francisco	21	Bombay	37
Amsterdam	14	Bungalore	22	Frankfurt	53
Helsinki, Paris	15	Moscow	23	Dublin	57
Rio de Janeiro	15	Lyon	25	Calcutta *	270

Small Firms Association, 2002. * Mostly on foot or by public transport.

PORRIDGE

3 CRITICISMS OF RTE'S COMEDY 'PATHS TO FREEDOM' BY INMATES OF MOUNTJOY PRISON

1. "*Paths to Freedom* doesn't reflect life inside or outside prison."
2. "The character Rats gives a wrong impression about life in prison."
3. "All the inmates believe that the programme should show what drugs do to people and the temptation they are to ex-prisoners while they are on the outside trying to go straight."

Evening Herald: 'Prisoners Find No Joy In TV Series' 29/11/2000.

THE VOICE OF IRISH FOOTBALL

"I was a young lad when I was growing up."
— *David O'Leary*

"We got on better with the likes of Holland, Belgium, Norway and Sweden, some of whom are not even in Europe."
— *Jack Charlton*

"I'd rather play in front of a full stadium than an empty crowd."
— *Johnny Giles*

"I was feeling as sick as the proverbial donkey."
— *Mick McCarthy*

"Collina is the only referee that, when he makes a decision, there's no arms thrown into the air and no gestating."
— *Niall Quinn*

"All strikers go through what they call a 'glut', where they don't score goals."
— *Mark Lawrenson*

FINE GAEL ANAGRAMS

ALAN DUKES	ALAS, NUKED
FINE GAEL LABOUR COALITION	*UNRELIABLE LOGICIAN AFOOT*
MICHAEL LOWRY	YO! I CHARM WELL

THE TRUTH ABOUT TV, 1961

"Whereas people had to go out of their homes to see movies, television can bring all this pagan propaganda into the family circle, with even more disastrous results. This is the big weapon of anti-Christian forces today. More souls may be taken away from Christ through the gospel of pleasure they absorb through TV, than if the anti-Christ would start an open bloody persecution in our country."

Catholic Truth Society, 1961. The CTS also claimed: "A baby was born in a taxi en route to the hospital, instead of in the hospital, because the mother couldn't tear herself away from her favourite programme."

LYRIC FM'S TOP 'LUNCHTIME CHOICES'

	Composers		*Top ten of the top hundred pieces 2003*	
1	J Strauss	1	Hard Times Come Again No More	Foster
2	Bizet	2	Time To Say Goodbye	Qarantotto
3	Mozart	3	Blue Danube Waltz	J Strauss
4	Gounod	4	Romance, from The Gadfly	Shostakovich
5	Romberg	5	Angels Guard Thee	Godard
6	Puccini	6	The Robins Return	Fisher
7	Mascagni	7	Elizabethan Serenade	Binge
8	Lehar	8	Spiegel Im Spiegel	Pärt
9	Grieg	9	Czardas	Monti
10	Vivaldi	10	Cavalleria Rusticana	Mascagni

THE EURO BANKNOTES

Note	*Colour*	*'Age & Style' Illustrated*	*Dimensions*
€ 5	Grey	Classical	120 x 62 mm
€ 10	Red	Romanesque	127 x 67 mm
€ 20	Blue	Gothic	133 x 72 mm
€ 50	Orange	Renaissance	140 x 77 mm
€ 100	Green	Baroque & Rococo	147 x 82 mm
€ 200	Yellow	Iron & Glass Architecture	153 x 82 mm
€ 500	Purple	20th Century Architecture	160 x 82 mm

Euro notes have pictures of windows, arches, gateways and bridges. 10 billion notes produced to replace national ones, nearly 5 billion more held in reserve.

DEF LEPPARD'S ADVERT

Placed in Hot Press *ahead of 1986 World Tour*

So! Dublin, we're off and wish to express our thanks to all of you who have helped us along over the last twelve months. Special thanks to Windmill for Studio II, all the wonderful clubs, restaurants… all those who broke into our cars, stole our bikes and robbed our apartments. C'est la vie! Non? We will be back.

THE NATIONAL WAY FORWARD
BY JUSTIN 'NO-TO-NICE' BARRETT

On Refugee Advocates:
"[They] are, almost to a man and woman, the abortion advocates, the contraception advocates, the Europhiles, the anti-Catholic bigots."

On paedophelia:
"In engaging in child abuse, a Catholic priest is acting… contrary to Catholic teaching. However, as a homosexual, his actions are consistent, and might lead the general public to draw certain conclusions concerning that so-called 'sexual orientation'."

On 'So-called Racism':
"Honesty rather than so-called 'racism' demands that it be stated clearly that the non-Europeans create the most intractable problem of all."

On Parliamentary Government:
"Foreign". "The party system ensures the rise of the basest of characters."

On Strong Government:
"Presidential democracy" would hand a directly elected leader the power to select "his" own cabinet.

Available from Guild Press, Spring, Granard, Co Longford (€14.00)

JACK CHARLTON'S ALL-IRELAND TEAM

Pat *Jennings*

Denis *Irwin* — Mick *McCarthy* — Paul *McGrath* — Steve *Staunton*

Ray *Houghton* — Roy *Keane* — Johnny *Giles* — George *Best*

Frank *Stapleton* — Gerry *Armstrong*

Best is the only Northern Ireland player about whom Jack had no reservations. He expressed extreme guilt about selecting Jennings ahead of Packie Bonnar, and selected Armstrong instead of John Aldridge "because I can't keep picking everyone from the Republic".

THE 7-PLUS WONDERS OF IRELAND

Sunday Tribune, 2001		*RTE Radio 1, 2003*
Newgrange	1	The Book of Kells
The Giant's Causeway	2	The Birr Castle Telescope
The Bog of Allen	3	Newgrange
Inis Mór	4	Valentia Fossil Footprints
The Rock of Cashel	5	Boyne Valley Viaduct
Skellig Michael	6	The Burren
The Cliffs of Moher	7	The Giant's Causeway
The River Shannon	8	The Casino at Marino
The Burren	9	
'Our Seven Wonders' by Nell McCafferty		*'Seven Wonders of Ireland' By Mary Mulvihill*

FIANNA FÁIL ANAGRAMS

LIAM LAWLOR	AMORAL WILL
CHARLES HAUGHEY	*HUSH! HEAR LEGACY*
EAMON DE VALERA	LOVED A MEAN ERA

AMERICAN TV LEPRECHAUNS

Lucky the Leprechaun starred in adverts for the cereal 'Lucky Charms', which came in heart, diamond, star, clover and other shapes. In 2000, Lucky Charms creator John Holahan and his wife died in a road accident while going to visit their dying daughter in hospital.

Leprechaun Hunters invaded the Ponderosa Ranch in a 1963 episode of 'Bonanza', after Hoss Cartwright rescued a little green-clad man from a bear and found a box of gold. It turned out to be the savings of a group of runaway circus performers.

Barney Killakilarney featured in a 1981 animation. *Dooley the Leprechaun* ruled The Land of Beyond in the 1950s show 'The Whistling Wizard'.

PIRATE RADIO STATIONS OF THE 1970s

AND THEIR BROADCASTING FREQUENCIES

Capitol Radio, Cork	253m	Atlantic Radio	300m
ARD, Dublin	257m	Radio Galway	199m
Big D Radio	273m	Radio Westcoast	219m
Radio Dublin	253m	Radio Cill Dara	270m
Radio Carousel	265m	Big L, Limerick	194m
Radio Dundalk	220m	Radio Suirside	257m

IRISH CONDOMS BEFORE "THE IRISH SOLUTION"

1960s: Promotion, sale, import of condoms is illegal (branded 'instruments of race suicide' by critics). Doctors prescribe the pill, *not* to prevent pregnancy but to regularize menstruation so women can use the Church-approved 'safe period'.

1969: Fertility Guidance Clinics in Dublin use legal loophole to give away free condoms while taking cash donations.

1970s: IRA bomb-makers use condoms in making explosive devices. Some 'republicans' are concerned about the morality of using condoms.

1971: Women's Lib Movement runs 'Contraceptive Train' to Belfast, while Taoiseach Jack Lynch doesn't want to "leave (condoms) on the long finger".

1973: Mary McGee court case. High Court says she can legally use contraceptives, just not buy them or import them. Supreme Court rules that constitutional right to privacy means a right to contraception.

1974: Taoiseach Liam Cosgrave votes against his own Govt's Family Planning Bill. Paddy Cooney tells Dáil that buying condoms "implies a right to fornicate and in my opinion there is no such natural right".

1979: UCD removes student-installed condom machine.

1979: CJ Haughey Health Act is "An Irish solution to an Irish problem": married couples can lawfully buy condoms, with a doctor's prescription, for 'bona fide family planning purposes'.

THE 'NEW' IRISH BANKNOTES, 1992-2002

Note	*Colour*	*Illustrations on Front and Back*		*First*
£5	Brown	F	Sr C McAuley, Mater Hospital	1994
		B	Schoolroom, three children study the poem 'Mise Raifteri an File'	
£10	Green	F	James Joyce, aerial view of Dublin	1992
		B	Liffey river god, map of Dublin, extract from *Finnegan's Wake*	
£20	Purple	F	D O'Connell, Derrynane Abbey	1992
		B	O'Connell's Pledge, Four Courts	
£50	Blue	F	D Hyde, Áras an Uachtaráin	1995
		B	Piper, Conradh na Gaeilge crest	
£100	Red	F	CS Parnell, Avondale House	1996
		B	Details from Parnell Monument	

McCauley: founder of Sisters of Mercy. Joyce: author. O'Connell: political leader. Hyde: first Irish President. Parnell: political leader.

VOTE SINN FÉIN

"We will not stop short of a 36-county Irish Republic.
We will settle for nothing less."
Francie Molloy hardens the traditional party stance.

Newsnight Presenter:
"I'm sure the leader of Sinn Féin would not make any outrageous remarks in the run-up to a general election."
SF Candidate Aengus O'Snodaigh:
"Oh yes, he certainly would."

Belfast woman on IRA decommissioning:
"I'm disgusted. I've always believed not a bullet, not an ounce.
Sinn Féin will never get my vote again."
Philip Boucher Hayes: "Who will get your vote?"
Woman: "Probably the Green Party."

"Hugging trees has a calming effect on me."
Gerry Adams

RADIO RAMBO

In May 1990, as Century Radio floundered, Communications Minister Ray Burke unveiled proposals to radically alter the content of 2FM. The pop station would, in future, provide: "Education and public information on continental languages, rural and farming sectors, business and trades union affairs, social welfare and social affairs advice." Alan Dukes responded in the Dáil that "a smell of sharp practice and corruption" surrounded "the whole sordid affair".

HIGHEST DIVORCE RATES OF PEOPLE WHOSE MARRIAGE HAS ENDED

Area	*Divorce Rate*	*Ended*	*Divorced*	*Separated*
Leitrim	47.8 %	906	433	473
Mayo	45.0 %	3,971	1,786	2,185
Kerry	45.0 %	5,068	2,279	2,789
Galway County	44.1 %	4,320	1,905	2,415
Roscommon	43.9 %	1,770	777	993

Census 2002. Separated includes deserted. State average is 36.4%.

THERE'S ONLY ONE JOHN ALDRIDGE

"There's only one club in Europe that you can leave Manchester United for — Real Madrid or Barcelona."

"Last week's match was a real game of cat and dog."

"If the fourth official had done his job correctly, it wouldn't have happened... but I don't want to blame anyone."

"It gets like this in Liverpool when you're on the ferry and the sun reflects off the Mersey." (On the Florida heat)

"Liverpool (have) given themselves a mountain to climb. In fact, they have to climb Everest, which is just around the corner from here." (In Basle, Switzerland.)

FIVE TRAINING TIPS FROM THE IRISH MOUNTAIN RACING ASSOCIATION

1. A 10k mountain race uses the effort of a 15k road race.
2. Strength & stamina going up, skill & agility going down.
3. Practice your descents on a soft, longish, grassy slope.
4. Technique: lean forward; land with slightly bent knees.
5. Practice descents sparingly; it is demanding on the body.

SPONSORED RADIO SHOWS OF THE 1950s

Transatlantic Call with Pat Layde	*Batchelors*
Bear Brand with Noel Andrews	*Bear Brand Stockings*
Brookfield Programme with Harry Thuillier	*Brookfield Sweets*
Stargazing with Eamonn Andrews	*Clarks Shoes*
Ladies Journal with Maxwell Sweeney	*The ESB*
Information Desk with Tom and Peggy	*Fruitfield Jam*
The Kennedys of Castleross with Godfrey Quigley	*Fry Cadbury*
The Dalys of Honeydew Farm with Ita Daly	*Gateaux*
Uncle Dan the Rambling Man with Philip O'Flynn	*Golden Vale*
Hovis Programme with Niall Boden	*Hovis Bread*
Murrays Programme with Harry Thuillier	*Murrays Car Rental*
Silvikrin Programme with Cecil Barror	*Silvikrin Shampoo*
Leisure Time with Harry Thuillier	*Tayto Crisps*
Waltons Programme with Leo Maguire	*Waltons Music Store*
The Planet Man with Gay Byrne	*Urney Chocolate*

Bear Brand: Music themed on brand names of stockings, e.g. Las Vegas, Ohio, Oklahoma.

Brookfield: "A mix of snipped, flipped, chipped, slipped and should-be-nipped records."

Golden Vale: Uncle Dan the Rambling Man plays music and talks to two children.

Hovis: Listeners send in their stories about honesty, bravery, animals and children.

Tayto: Assortment of relaxing music. Listeners are invited to "Take it easy with Tayto".

Urney: "Your Planet Man host is Gay Byrne, who presents a spaceship serial on disc."

ORDER DECLARING THE IRA ILLEGAL

"The association styling itself the Irish Republican Army (also the IRA and Óglaigh na hÉireann) is, in the opinion of the Executive Council, an unlawful association… This order may be cited for all purposes as the Constitution (Declaration of Unlawful Association) Order, 1936."
— *Gerald Boland*, Minister for Justice, 18 June 1936.

RELIGIOUS READERSHIPS, 1973

The Far East	194,000	*The Brief*	31,000
The Word	170,000	*Star of the East*	26,000
Africa	160,000	*The Cross*	25,000
Mission Outlook	75,000	*Salesian Bulletin*	25,000
Reality	55,000	*Catholic Standard*	21,000
Caritas	50,000	*St Vincent de Paul*	16,000
African Missionary	45,000	*St Anthony's Annals*	15,000
Daystar	44,000	*Tidings*	9,000
The Irish Catholic	40,000	*The Fold*	9,000
The Pioneer	40,000	*The Furrow*	8,000

Combined 1m+; compared to 871,000 for top 20 non-religious magazines.

FOUR WAYS TO GET ELECTED

1932: Ride a White Horse

De Valera entered towns astride white charger flanked by parade of pitchforks.

1943: Get On Your Bike

Cycle with sandwich board: 'Here Comes Oliver' (front); 'There Goes Flanagan' (back).

1977: Add Some Colour

Albert Reynolds introduced colour posters to the Irish electorate. Elected!

1981: Change Your Name

Sean Loftus added 'Dublin Bay' by deed poll, moved up the ballot paper, won seat.

SOME BIRDS OF IRELAND

Arctic Skua	Grey Phalarope	Sedge Warbler
Bar-tailed Godwit	Little Grebe	Stonechat
Cirl Bunting	Nightjar	Twite
Egyptian Goose	Pomarine Skua	Velvet Scoter
Fulmar	Rednecked Grabe	Waxwing
Gadwall	Ring Ouzel	Wheatear
Greenshank	Sanderling	Wigeon

WHERE TO MEET AN IRISH SPEAKER WHO NEVER SPEAKS IRISH

Most			*Least*
Waterford City	34.0 %	Donegal	18.5 %
Dublin City	32.7 %	Galway County	19.5 %
Fingal	32.6 %	Kerry	24.2 %
Dun Laoghaire	32.2 %	Galway City	24.6 %
Cork City	31.9 %	Mayo	25.5 %

Census 2002. Percentage of Irish speakers who say they never speak Irish.

COMPARISONS OF THE DÁIL WITH THE MUPPET SHOW

Michael McDowell	PD	2002	Tribunal into Donegal Gardaí
Dermot Ahern	FF	2001	Order of business
Mairín Quill	PD	1997	Financing of local government
Jim Higgins	FG	1995	Amendment to standing orders
Jim Kemmy	Lab	1993	Dáil reform
Alan Shatter	FG	1991	Financial resolutions
John Wilson	FF	1979	Order of business
John Kelly	FG	1979	Management of the economy
Michael O'Leary	Lab	1979	Restoration of food subsidies

After a barren decade in the 80s, Muppet references are making a comeback.

'67 REASONS WHY CONDOMS SPREAD AIDS'

In 1991 the Children's Protection Society circulated this expensively-produced booklet to all TDs and Senators. The 67 reasons, which were "compiled with eminent medical assistance", included:

"The more condoms that are sold against AIDS, the more AIDS is transmitted": A 10% failure rate means every 1,000 condoms sold causes 100 more "actions open to AIDS".

Richard Branson is "the first since independence" to get the Irish Govt "to make our laws like his own country's… Who is this epoch-making man?"

If a man with AIDS has sex with his wife, she will die at age 35. If he uses condoms, she will still die at age 41. Only abstaining because he loves her will allow her to live to 79.

Cavan-Monaghan "has either Europe's lowest or the world's lowest AIDS rate, depending on sources… How?" Answer: Not a single Carrickmacross trader will sell condoms.

'Religious belief is historically the only successful basis for the rule of law, and this is a vital factor in preventing, notably, sexual assaults on children."

Plus: "There is no active role for women in condom sex"; The 'Power of Dreams' rock group promotes condoms; "In a debate, the condom lobby would lose."

ISBN 0951769804. An *Irish Times* letter looked forward to such follow-ups as '67 Reasons Why Crash-Helmets Spread Motorbike Accidents'.

LEAST STABLE IRISH MARRIAGES

Area	*Failure Rate*	*Still Married*	*Divorced*	*Separated*
Limerick City	14.4 %	16,915	787	2,031
Dublin City	13.6 %	148,311	7,354	15,555
Galway City	13.3 %	18,619	1,090	1,708
Waterford City	12.0 %	15,783	678	1,443
Wicklow	11.5 %	44,319	2,187	3,474

Census 2002. State average is 9.8%. Separated includes deserted.

LETTERS SENT TO TAOISIGH

Seán Lemass, 1965: "What I want to ask you, dear Premier, is if the women and girls in Catholic Ireland are wearing 'minnie dresses' and tight pants and 'minnie skirts'? Here in the USA our women in their 'minnie dresses' have brought God's displeasure. We have had storms. Earthquakes…"

'The Hon' Jack Lynch, 1972: "When I visited Ireland in 1967 many Protestants told me that it was most difficult for a Protestant young man to get a job in S Ireland. Of course, my father, having been brought up in Ireland, was a religious bigot, and I'm sure the relatives I met were also."

Liam Cosgrave, 1973: "Dear Liam, contraception is an evil which has beset mankind for as far back as history records… Those who try to frighten people with demographic arguments should know that the whole population of the world could fit into the wee county of Louth."

To Lemass from Maud Sullivan of Los Angeles; to Lynch from an American Citizen; to Cosgrave from Rev Dr Richard Mulcahy.

THE FIANNA FÁIL PRESS GANG

1931: De Valera founds *Irish Press.* Motto: 'The Truth In News.' Dev flogs 200,000 £1 ordinary shares to FF faithful. Neglects to mention 200 secret 'B' shares making *Press* his private property.

1968: Dispute with teachers' union. Education Min Brian Lenihan gets Dept official to write letters to papers, 'signed' by 'readers'. Story leaks. Min says pressing the matter would jeopardise deal with unions.

1984: Internal party circular instructs: "Stories that might be incriminating to opposition deputies or councillors should be fully checked and forwarded to the Press Officer." News leaks. Circular withdrawn.

2002: Officer with Govt Information Service poses as member of public on Gerry Ryan Show. 'Brian' explains why Bertie Ahern was spot-on to make Ray Burke Justice Minister in 1997.

SELECTED DATES FROM CJ HAUGHEY'S GUBU GOVERNMENT, 1982

Feb 18th: General election. Pat O'Connor, CJ's election agent, enters two voting booths with ballot papers. Charged with double voting; not proven to have voted even once.

March 30th: Haughey gives top EEC job to Fine Gael TD Dick Burke, and plans to win ensuing by-election.

May 10th: Justice Minister Sean Doherty begins unlawful tapping of journalist Bruce Arnold's phone.

May 17th: Justice Minister Doherty stars in lavish law & order TV campaign.

May 24th: On eve of Dublin West by-election, Env Minister Ray Burke has new trees planted there, fulfilling wishes expressed by voters.

May 25th: Fianna Fail loses by-election caused by Euro gift to FG. Next day, new trees mysteriously vanish from Dublin West constituency.

May 27th: Unlawful tapping begins of journalist Geraldine Kennedy's phone.

Aug 13th: Murder suspect Malcolm McArthur arrested in home of Haughey's Attorney General, Patrick Connolly.

Sept 22nd: Garda car on protection detail with Doherty crashes. Car, pistol and Uzi machine gun left unattended.

Oct 21st: Tánaiste Ray McSharry secretly tapes chat with resigned Education Minister, Martin O'Donoghue.

Dec 14th: Fine Gael's Garret Fitzgerald elected Taoiseach.

GUBU coined by Conor Cruise O'Brien when Haughey described McArthur arrest as 'Grotesque', 'Unprecedented', 'Bizarre', 'Unbelievable'.

TODAY FM RAISES THE DEAD

"No rape, abuse or murder victims were interviewed during the research."
— *Newsdesk*

"And has the court heard from the victim today?"
— *Eamon Dunphy* covers the Nevin murder case

2FM'S TOP TEN IRISH SONGS, EVER!

1	*The Boys are Back in Town*	Thin Lizzy
2	*One*	U2
3	*Teenage Kicks*	The Undertones
4	*Rat Trap*	The Boomtown Rats
5	*The Town I Loved So Well*	Luke Kelly
6	*Celebrate*	An Emotional Fish
7	*Brown Eyed Girl*	Van Morrison
8	*Parachute*	Something Happens
9	*The Voyage*	Christy Moore
10	*Nothing Compares 2U*	Sinead O'Connor

Broadcast on Saint Patrick's Day 2003.

EUROPEAN UNION ANAGRAMS

EUROSCEPTICS	IS SECRET COUP
EUROPEAN PARLIAMENT	*APPEAL REMUNERATION*
PAT COX MEP	EXACT POMP

THE 'NEW MONEY' IRISH COINS, 1971-2002

Coin	*New Value*	*In 'Old Money'*	*Reverse*	*Front*
½p	Halfpenny	1.2 pence	Celtic bird	Harp
1p	Penny	2.4 pence	Celtic bird	Harp
2p	Two pence	4.8 pence	Celtic bird	Harp
5p	Five pence	One shilling	Bull	Harp
10p	Ten pence	Two shillings	Salmon	Harp
20p	Twenty pence	Four shillings	Horse	Harp
50p	Fifty pence	Ten shillings	Woodcock	Harp
£1	One pound	One pound	Stag	Harp

5p and 10p introduced 1969; ½p, 1p, 2p, 50p 1971. ½p phased out, 20p introduced 1986. £1 introduced 1990. Smaller 5p and 10p minted 1993 with animals facing left, same as on other coins.

FOUR ESSENTIAL IRISH STATUTORY INSTRUMENTS

Sweets and Chocolates (Maximum Prices) Orders (Revocation) Order, 1952. Revoked maximum prices on sweets and chocolate set by Emergency Powers (Sweets & Chocolates) (Maximum Prices) Order, 1943 (Amendment) (No. 2) Order, 1947.

Standard Specification (Finished Wallpaper) Order, 1953. Set the national standard for finished wallpaper to be 11.5 yards long and 21 inches wide (plus six other specifications). One roll from every sixty to be selected at random to test conformity.

Imposition of Duties (No 177) (Crown Corks and Artificial Plastic Footballs) Order, 1968. Imposed custom duty of 16% on crown corks, and of 48% (full) and 44% (preferential and special preferential) on certain non-UK plastic footballs.

Imposition of Duties (Anti-Dumping Duty on Pencils) Order, 1977. Imposed an anti-dumping duty of £1.49 per gross on wood-cased pencils produced in (or originating in) Czechoslovakia, and classified at tariff code numbers 9805-416 and 9805-424.

TOP TWENTY NAMES OF IRISH BOYS AND GIRLS

Registered in Ireland in 2002

Boys				*Girls*			
Jack	868	Dylan	485	Sarah	655	Megan	387
Sean	866	Aaron	467	Aoife	585	Hannah	368
Adam	798	Patrick	366	Ciara	577	Rachel	364
Conor	748	Ryan	365	Emma	532	Rebecca	361
James	581	John	362	Chloe	516	Leah	351
Daniel	559	Eoin	361	Amy	485	Laura	349
Cian	536	Matthew	351	Katie	418	Jessica	302
Michael	520	Thomas	349	Niamh	407	Kate	301
David	501	Ben	345	Sophie	404	Emily	278
Luke	489	Joshua	345	Lauren	402	Caoimhe	272

CELTIC GODS & THEIR PORTFOLIOS

God	Portfolio	God	Portfolio
Aengus Óg	Love, Youth	Donn	The Dead
Banba	Fertility, War	Epona	Horses, Cattle
Bel	Agriculture	Eriu	Irishness
Brigid	Poets, Fertility	Goibhniu	Alcohol
Creidhne	Metalworking	Lir	The Sea
Cu Roi	Sorcery	Luchtaine	Carpentry
Cyhiraeth	Streams	Lugh	The Sun
Dagda	Supreme God	Morrigan	War
Danu	Mother God	Nuada	King of Erin
Dian Cécht	Healing	Ogma	Eloquence

EARLY IRISH OLYMPIANS

Athens, 1896. Dubliner John Pius Boland wins Ireland's first gold medal, in tennis. For years, this win is wrongly attributed to USA or Britain.

St Louis, 1904. Tom Kiely wins gold in the 'All-Round Championship'. Again, for years, this is wrongly attributed to USA or Britain.

Paris, 1924. French customs officers discover a gun in the luggage of Irish footballer Ernie Crawford. It is, he insists, "for peace of mind".

Paris, 1924. Jack Yeats wins a silver medal for his painting, 'Swimming'. Oliver St John Gogarty wins bronze for his 'Ode to the Tailteann Games'.

Amsterdam, 1928. Doctor Pat O'Callaghan wins gold in the hammer throw, as Ireland keeps women competitors at home at the Vatican's behest.

Los Angeles, 1932. Ceylon-born Bob Tisdall wins a gold for Ireland in the 400 metres hurdles, despite never having run the event until that year.

London, 1948. At the opening parade, the 'Ireland' delegation lines up behind Iraq. They are told they must compete as 'Éire', lining up behind Egypt.

Helsinki, 1952. Following the 'Éire/Ireland' row in 1948, the 'Irish Olympic Council' has changed its name to 'Olympic Council of Ireland'.

WHEN HARE MET THE DISTRICT JUSTICE

In June 1973, five members of the Hare Krishna religion were charged in Dublin District Court after their singing upset some passers-by. The Judge sent the tangerine-clad revellers on their way with the following admonishment: "Why are you dressed in those ridiculous garments? I could sentence you to contempt for wearing a scarf like that… I can warn you, you were lucky not to have been assaulted by the crowd. Any decent Irishman would object to this carry-on… My only regret is that I can't have you locked up."

THE 'OLD' IRISH BANKNOTES, 1976-1996

Note	*Colour*	*Front*	*Back*	*Last*
£1	Green	Queen Medbh	Book of Dun Cow	1989
£5	Brown	John Scotus Eriugena	Book of Kells	1993
£10	Purple	Dean Swift	Map of Dublin	1992
£20	Blue	WB Yeats	Blasket Islands	1992
£50	Brown	T O'Carolan	Musical Instruments	1991
£100	Green	Lady Lavery	River God	1977

Medbh: mythical queen. Scotus: medieval philosopher. Swift: 18th Century author. Yeats: 20th Century poet. O'Carolan: 18th Century harpist. Lavery: lady with harp on the pre-1979 £100 note, which continued in circulation as the new notes did not include a £100 note.

VISIONARY IDEAS FROM GAY MITCHELL TD

1. Bring the 2004 Olympic Games to Dublin 1992
2. Establish a Minister for Law and Order 1987
3. Establish an Oireachtas Medal of Honour 1986
4. 9-5 working day and shorter holidays for judges 1986
5. Make criminals work down the sewers 1985

SNAP HAPPY

MINISTERIAL EXPENDITURE ON PHOTOS, 2002

Minister	*Department*	*Spend*
McDaid/O'Donoghue	Arts/Sports/Tourism	€ 41,874
Bertie Ahern	Taoiseach	€ 30,940
Charlie McCreevy	Finance	€ 27,238
Joe Walsh	Agriculture	€ 26,007
Michael Smith	Defence	€ 1,227

Smith's was the lowest spend. A single issue of The *Longford News*

CREATIVE THINKING

RESPONSES BY ADVERTISERS TO COMPLAINTS MADE TO THE ADVERTISING STANDARDS AUTHORITY OF IRELAND

Coors Light: Young men drink late into the night, then frolic in the snow in their underwear. Advertiser claims that the advert encourages responsible behaviour, because drinking gradually all night is better than packing drinks in before closing time.

Baileys: A man, kissed in the dark, tastes Baileys. Checks out women who are drinking it. Another man raises a glass of Baileys and everyone laughs. Advertiser argues they were laughing at the man's general confusion, not because he may have been kissed by a man.

FM104: Poster shows slogan 'Hit Hot Music' with letter 'S', partially obscured, in front of the word 'Hit'. Another reads 'King Brilliant Music', preceded by a partially visible letter 'C'. Advertiser claims slogans could be 'It's Hit Hot Music' and 'Kicking Brilliant Music'.

Housing Development: Ad states that Tullow is only 42 miles and 45 minutes from Dublin. Complainant says it is actually 48 miles and 1 hour 22 minutes. Advertiser counters that distance was calculated from Tullow to Tallaght, which is in Dublin.

The complaint against Baileys was rejected, the three others upheld.

IRELAND'S MOST-CAPPED WORLD CUP FINALISTS

9—Packie
Bonnar

6—Gary *Kelly*	5—Mick *McCarthy*	5—Kevin *Moran*	13—Steve *Staunton*
9—Ray *Houghton*	9—Paul *McGrath*	9—Andy *Townsend*	5—Kevin *Sheedy*
	3 (+3)—Niall *Quinn*	6 (+2)—John *Aldridge*	

Italy 1990		*USA 1994*		*Japan 2002*	
Packie Bonnar	5	Packie Bonnar	4	Shay Given	4
Chris Morris	5	Irwin/Kelly	2	Steve Finnan	3
Paul McGrath	5	Phil Babb	4	Gary Breen	4
Mick McCarthy	5	Paul McGrath	4	Steve Staunton	4
Steve Staunton	5	Terry Phelan	3	Ian Harte	4
Ray Houghton	5	Ray Houghton	4	Gary Kelly	4
Kevin Moran	5	Roy Keane	4	Mark Kinsella	4
Andy Townsend	5	Andy Townsend	4	Matt Holland	4
Kevin Sheedy	5	Steve Staunton	4	Kevin Kilbane	4
John Aldridge	5	John Sheridan	4	Robbie Keane	4
Niall Quinn	3	Tommy Coyne	3	Damien Duff	4
Tony Cascarino	2	Aldridge/McAteer	1	Jason McAteer	1

Substitutes: 3 — T Cascarino, J McAteer, S Reid, N Quinn
2 — J Aldridge, K Cunningham, A McLoughlin, R Whelan
1 — D Connolly, S Finnan, D Kelly, D O'Leary, J Sheridan

TV3 TELLS IT AS IT IS

"There is a feeling that you have to make it abroad to be accepted at home, which is rubbish, but at the same time there is an element of truth in that."
— *Aidan Cooney* to the band 6

"Bringing you back to the North, there's big developments happening there with the news last night that there's big developments happening there."
— *Ireland AM Presenter*

RTE'S NEWS AT ONE

"Those people who've been killed have a lot of scores to settle, and they'll be anxious to settle them."
— *Richard Downes*

"I'm particularly thrilled for the young people… and for all the older people."
— *Wexford hurling manager*

"The Taoiseach has determined that during the lifetime of this Dail there will be an abortion on the referendum issue."
— *David McCullough*

"If Base Camp 10 is the top of the mountain we're at Base Camp 9."
— *GAA manager*

CABINET CONFIDENTIALITY

1990: Former Govt Minister Gemma Hussey publishes her cabinet diaries. "The room needed a coat of paint and there were dull paintings on the wall." Tensions were eased by "Jim Mitchell's occasional pranks, Ruairí Quinn's cartoons and John Boland's uproarious Dublin yarns".

1992: Ray Burke, CJ Haughey, Albert Reynolds etc. to be quizzed at Beef Tribunal about role in scandal whereby Irish taxpayers were liable to pay £180m to Saddam Hussein.

1992: Attorney General, with at least tacit say-so of Govt, seeks a court ruling that it is unconstitutional to ask what goes on in cabinet. Fine Gael calls the move "disgraceful".

1992: High Court judge rules against the AG, saying that if corruption occurred in cabinet, such a ruling would prevent uncovering of guilt where it existed. Would also place Govt's rights above those of people. AG appeals decision.

1992: On appeal, Supreme Court rules for confidentiality. The practice continues after each cabinet meeting of briefing the government press secretary, who then briefs the political correspondents. No arrests are made.

1996: Taoiseach John Bruton revises FG position, saying he wouldn't favour "a major change in constitutional practices maintained in this country for a long time".

DUNPHY ON EURO '88

"Assumptions made last week about the validity of our claim to a place alongside the best in Europe have been proved correct this week. Too much credit ought not accrue to your humble correspondent." (Translation: "I was wrong.")

THE MOST IRISH PARTS OF LONDON

District	*Pop*	*Irish*	*%*
Brent	263,464	18,313	7.0
Islington	175,797	10,057	5.7
Hammersmith and Fulham	165,242	7,983	4.8
Ealing	300,948	14,285	4.7
Luton	184,371	8,569	4.6
Camden	198,020	9,149	4.6
Harrow	206,814	9,057	4.4
Haringey	216,507	9,302	4.3

Census 2001. Irish means ethnicity, not necessarily country of birth.

COMMEMORATIVE IRISH COINS

1966 — 10 shillings
50 years since Easter rising.
Cúchulainn and Pearse.

1988 — 50 pence
1,000 years since Dublin founded. Shield of Dublin.

1990 — ECU Set
Irish Presidency of EC.
50, 10 & 5 ECU coins.

1997 — £1
50 years of United Nations.
Dove, UN Logo, 1945-1995.

2000 — £1
1,000 years since 1000 AD.
Ancient 'Broighter boat'.

2002 — Euro Set
Ireland joining Euro.
Mint set of eight coins.

Dublin was actually founded (and producing coins) before 988.
UN coin not put into circulation; produced 1997, dated 1995.

PEOPLE WHO 'OBSTRUCTED AND HINDERED' THE FLOOD TRIBUNAL

Michael Bailey	Builder	*Raphael Burke*, TD 1973–97; Dublin Cllr 1967–78, Chair 1985–87; Min of State 1978–80; Minister for Environment 1980–81, 1982; for Energy & Communications* 1987–88; for Communications*, Industry & Commerce 1988–89; for Justice & Communications* 1989–91; for Justice 1991–92; for Foreign Affairs 1997.
Tom Bailey	Builder	
Oliver Barry	Promoter	
Tom Brennan	Builder	
John Finnegan	Auctioneer	
PJ Mara	Consultant	
Joe McGowan	Builder	
Joseph Murphy Jnr	Builder	
Joseph Murphy Snr	Builder	
James Stafford	Hotelier	

* Burke repeatedly retained Communications portfolio when moving Ministries.

HISTORY AND GEOGRAPHY

"When I was in primary school we had a drawing on the wall of Northern Ireland with blue surrounding it. I thought Northern Ireland was an island until I was twelve."

— Anne Dunlop, *The Pineapple Tart*

IRELAND'S FIRST GOLF CLUB?

The Golfing Union of Ireland lists the first Irish golf clubs as Royal Belfast (1881), Curragh and Fota Island (1883), Royal Dublin (1885) and Mornington (1886). However, an advert in *Faulkner's Dublin Journal* of 23 Oct 1762 announces: "The goff club meet to dine at the house of Mr Charles Moran at Bray on Thursday 28 October, at half an hour after three o'clock." Elias J Butts Esq was the chairman. Another article refers to "that manly game called goff" being played on a common, now the seafront promenade area of Bray.

PLATINUM LOGIC

"It's a dreadful disappointment, but the players have nothing to be disappointed about." — Martin O'Neill after a Celtic UEFA Cup defeat.

"He said that he'd give me the two jackets free if I bought one of them." — Caller to Radio 1's Liveline.

"(This) has increased the public representatives' lobby for decisive action against gangland killings by the Government and Gardaí." — *Northside People.*

OH, MISTER AMBASSADOR

William Fitzgerald was George Bush Senior's 83-year-old Ambassador to Ireland. In 1992 US Senators quizzed him on how the Maastricht referendum would go. "It's already done," he said. "On June 18th the referendum was held and 65% of the people supported it. 11% opposed it." Senator Joe Biden was puzzled. "But today is only June 3rd," he said. "Thank you for correcting me," said Fitzgerald. "I was in anticipation." (He was almost correct: 69% later voted yes.)

THE MOST IRISH PARTS OF ENGLAND

District	*Pop*	*Irish*	*%*
Luton	184,371	8,569	4.6
Manchester	392,819	14,826	3.8
Coventry	300,848	10,401	3.5
Inner London	2,766,114	93,164	3.4
Birmingham	977,087	31,467	3.2
Outer London	4,405,977	127,324	2.9
Watford	79,726	2,304	2.9
Trafford	210,145	5,874	2.8

Census 2001. Irish means ethnicity, not necessarily country of birth.

STRANGE EXCHANGES

RTE Reporter: "So everything was done that could be done?" *Eye Witness:* "Oh, more than everything."

Eamon Dunphy: "Sinéad O'Connor had a hit with Nothing Compares 2U. Who wrote it?" *Quiz Contestant:* "Jimmy McCarthy!"

Gareth O'Callaghan: "What is the singer Donna Summer's real name?" *Quiz Contestant:* "Mary Banotti!"

Larry Gogan: "Which fairytale character said: 'All the better to see you with, my dear'?" *Just a Minute Quiz Contestant:* "Was it Bruce Forsythe?"

BESTSELLING IRISH MAGAZINES, 1973

Magazine	Sales
The Dublin Post	120,000
Woman's Way	89,000
Old Moore's Almanac	88,000
RTE Guide	84,000
Irish Farmers Journal	69,000
United Irishman	65,000
Woman's Choice	49,000
New Spotlight	42,000
Ireland of the Welcomes	35,000
Irish Countrywoman	29,000
This Week	28,000
Gaelic Sport	28,000
Our Boys	26,000
Hibernia	19,000
Inniu	18,000
Biatas	18,000
Young Citizen	18,000
Distributive Worker	16,000
Car Buyer	15,000
Motoring Life	15,000

Combined 871,000; compared to 1m+ for top 20 religious publications.

STAR PROFILE, MUSICAL GAZETTE, 1971

"Donie Cassidy, aged 23, 5' 10", blue eyes, red hair, is a trumpeter with the Firehouse. He drives a Capri (very fast) and is in the habit of picking up parking tickets at the rate of one a week. His hobbies include fishing, hurling, horse racing, dog racing and speculation on the stock exchange. Endowed with the gift of the gab, he'd talk a hole through a wall!"

ME SIR, ME SIR, ASK ME SIR!

THE TEN MOST FREQUENT PANELISTS ON RTE'S QUESTIONS & ANSWERS, 2001-2003

Panelist	*Position*	*Apps*	*Last*
Michael McDowell	PD, Minister for Justice	5	May 03
Mary Hanafin	FF, Govt Chief Whip	4	Jun 03
Richard Bruton	FG, Deputy Leader	4	May 03
Willie O'Dea	FF, Minister of State	4	May 03
Micheál Martin	FF, Minister for Health	3	Jun 03
Joan Burton	Labour, TD	3	Jun 03
Joe O'Toole	Ind, Senator	3	May 03
Alison O'Connor	*Irish Independent* Journalist	3	May 03
John Waters	*Irish Times* Columnist	3	Mar 03
Mary Coughlan	FF, Minister for Family Affairs	3	Apr 03

From seasons Sep 2001-June 2002 and Sep 2002-Jun 2003.

IRELAND'S FIRST FIVE UK NUMBER 1 ALBUMS

Val Doonican Rocks, But Gently	Val Doonican	3 wks	1967
Back to Front	Gilbert O'Sullivan	1 wk	1973
War	U2	1 wk	1983
The Unforgettable Fire	U2	1 wk	1984
The Joshua Tree	U2	2 wks	1987

Guinness Book of British Hit Albums. Waterford's Val Doonican knocked The Beatles' 'Sergeant Pepper' off the top spot.

FIRST ST PATRICK'S DAY PARADE

The first to parade on St Patrick's Day to express pride in their Irish identity were 18th Century British soldiers stationed in New York. Military units were part of the NY parade until 1774. Irish-American soldiers paraded from 1783-1812, after which Irish-American civilian organisations took charge.

TWO PARLIAMENTARY OATHS

"...That the sacrifice of the mass, and the invocation of the blessed Virgin Mary, and other saints, as now practiced in the church of Rome, are impious and idolatrous..."
— *Oath for MPs, 1800s*

"I, (state name), do solemnly swear true faith and allegiance to the Constitution of the Irish Free State as by law established, and that I will be faithful to HM King George V, his heirs and successors by law, in virtue of the common citizenship of Ireland with Great Britain and her adherence to and membership of the group of nations forming the British Commonwealth of Nations."
— *Oath for TDs, 1920s*

IRISH MEDIA ANAGRAMS

THE PAT KENNY SHOW	HE'S WONKY, THEN APT
HOT PRESS MAGAZINE	*THE AMAZING POSERS*
MARIAN FINUCANE SHOW	HUMAN FACE WINS ON AIR

SO NEAR, YET SO FAR

THE LEAST IRISH PARTS OF ENGLAND

District	*Pop*	*Irish*	*%*
Northumberland National Park	1,934	0	0.00
Easington	93,995	126	0.13
Blyth Valley	81,266	152	0.19
Chester-le-Street	53,693	105	0.20
Wansbeck	61,138	126	0.21
Wear Valley	61,339	127	0.21
South Tyneside	152,785	365	0.24
Durham	493,470	1,254	0.25
Sedgefield	87,206	229	0.26
Hartlepool	88,611	235	0.27

Census 2001. Irish means ethnicity, not necessarily country of birth.

FEAR OF MUSIC

FR JOHN O'CONNOR'S GUIDE TO ROCK

"The term rock'n'roll comes from the gutter. It means fornicating in a car."

The Stones' 'Goats Head Soup' asks kids to behead goats and drink blood.

'Stairway To Heaven' played backwards is a prayer to "sweet Satan".

'Another One Bites The Dust' backwards is "Decide to smoke marijuana".

(From *Outlook*, magazine of the Holy Ghost Missions)

IT'S A FUNNY OLD GAME

1970s: FAI organises friendly games in Poland. Officials enjoy 'night life'. Players travel to one game in train luggage carriage. Officials relax on seats.

1980: Eoin Hand beats Paddy Mulligan to manager's job by one swing vote because board member thinks Mulligan threw a bun at him on an away trip.

1986: Jack Charlton becomes manager by accident (see p 56). Sends squad list to FAI. Finds FAI official is adding players that he likes onto the list.

1994: World Cup, Orlando. FAI sells tickets to commercial agents, including 'George the Greek'. Ends up with a 'trading shortfall' of £110,000.

1999: FAI announces plan to spend £65m on new 45,000-seat stadium. Forgets to include the £16m cost of site. Plan is shelved in 2001.

2002: World Cup, Saipan. FAI forgets to bring footballs to an island that has no pitch. Back home, FAI orders independent investigation into itself.

2002: FAI sells TV rights to subscription channel Sky. Govt says EU law protects cultural events. FAI says Irish football is not culturally important.

2002: Bid to host Euro 2008. UEFA panel is photographed at site of non-existent stadium and at Croke Park beside 'Do Not Walk on the Grass' sign.

Following the 2002 Genesis Report, the FAI has undergone a regime change.

THOSE WERE THE DAYS

"The surroundings of the dance hall, withdrawal from the hall for intervals, and back ways home have been the destruction of virtue in every part of Ireland." — *Catholic Bishops Conference, 1925*

"If your girls do not obey you, if they are not in at the hours appointed, lay the lash upon their backs. That was the good old system, and that should be the system today." — *Bishop O'Doherty of Galway, 1927*

ILLUSTRATIONS ON EURO COINS

Country	*Designs*	*Main Features Illustrated on Designs*
Austria	8	Von Sutner, Mozart, 3 buildings, 3 flowers
Belgium	1	King Albert II plus monogram with crown
Finland	3	Cloudberries, flying swans, heraldic lion
France	3	Tree with French motto, sower, Marianne
Germany	3	German eagle, Brandenburg Gate, oak twig
Greece	8	Spartan mosaic, owl, 3 politicians, 3 boats
Ireland	1	Celtic harp, word Éire (design Jarlath Hayes)
Italy	8	Significant portraits, sculptures and buildings
Luxembourg	1	His Royal Highness the Grand Duke Henri
Netherlands	2	Both designs feature Queen Beatrix
Portugal	3	All three designs feature Royal Seal of 1142
Spain	3	King Carlos I, Cervantes, Santiago Cathedral

There are eight Euro coins: €2, €1, 50c, 20c, 10c, 5c, 2c, 1c. Each is valid in any Euro country. The front has a map of Europe and the coin's value. The reverse, in each country, has one or more designs chosen by that Govt.

THREE IRISH FOUNDERS OF FOREIGN NAVIES

John Barry	Wexfordman	United States Navy
William Browne	Mayoman	Argentine Navy
Bernardo O'Higgins	Son of a Meathman	Chilean Navy

THE FIRST TEN LAWS OF THE IRISH FREE STATE

Constitution Act 1922	Adopting the Free State Constitution
Adapting Enactments	Updating references in old Statutes
Appropriation Act	£38,051,086 for financial year 1922-23
Local Elections	Postponing local elections due in 1923
Continuation Act	Continuing certain laws that were expiring
C & AG Act	Appointing Comptroller & Auditor-General
Indemnity Act	For British military activity 1916-23
Continuance of Charges	Maintaining transportation charges
Enforcement of Law	Giving powers of seizure to Sheriffs
Griffith Settlement	£1,000 a year to Arthur Griffith's widow

First five 1922; next five 1923. Appropriation Act enabled budget by allowing Finance Min to borrow or raise that sum. Indemnity Act ruled out legal actions against British military for any acts done in Ireland from 1916-1923.

THE SIMPSONS

TEN IRISH CAMEOS

Flanders' Vegas wife wants him to 'Irish up the coffee'. (Flanders says they do not use the 'I-word' in their house.)

Mr Burns once crippled an Irishman with a bumper car.

Michael Finn from the Green Potato Pub at O'Hare International Airport enters the Duff bartender competition.

Willie's rival is the drunken poet Groundskeeper Seamus.

Apu and his backup dancers do Riverdance at a disco.

Barney sings 'Tura-lura-loo' in an Irish accent.

Ralph has a Blarney Stone and sees a leprechaun.

Itchy & Scratchy show: 'Itchy Runs Afoul of an Irishman'.

U2 appear as guest stars in the 200th special episode.

An Irishwoman says that MASH's Mike Farrell 'really boils her potato'.

SELF AID CONCERT, DUBLIN, 1986

—Line Up—

Auto da Fe
Bagatelle
Big Self
Blue in Heaven
Boomtown Rats
Paul Brady
Cactus World News
The Chieftains
Clannad
Chris de Burgh
De Dannan
Elvis Costello & the Attractions
The Fountainhead
Rory Gallagher
In Tua Nua
Les Enfants
Christy Moore
Moving Hearts
Those Nervous Animals
The Pogues
Scullion
Brush Shields
Stockton's Wing
Chris Rea
U2
Van Morrison
Freddie White

'ADVERTISING WITH NOTHING TO SELL'

This was an Irish ad industry conference at Dublin's Central Hotel in 1943: rationing during 'The Emergency' left little to sell and colour ads were banned. Visits to Dr Stephen's VD clinic had shot from 15,000 (1941) to 26,000, raising industry hopes of a public info campaign on STDs, but Dev's Govt again adopted a 'Don't Mention The War' policy.

IRISH NAME-CHANGES

From	*To*
Bart Ahearne	Bertie Ahern
Tom Dudley	Bang Bang
David Evans	The Edge
Anto Fagan	Tony Fenton
Paul Hewson	Bono
Eithne Ní Bhraonáin	Enya
Adele King	Twink
Rigid Tool *	Ridge Tool
John Byrne	Hugh Leonard
Tony Gareth	Gareth O'Callaghan
Graham Walker	Graham Norton
Declan McManus	Elvis Costello
Pat Rabbitte	** Pet Rabbit
Rosemary Brown	Dana
Gerry Reynolds	Scott Williams
Sean Sherrard	Johnny Logan

* Rigid Tool: a Cork-based US firm that was persuaded to change its name.
** Pat Rabbitte pronounced 'Pet Rabbit' by Australian presenter on TV3.

GOING THAT EXTRA MILE (PER HOUR)

90-115 mph. John O'Donoghue 2001

Justice Minister absent from his speeding State car. He'd loaned it to family members to attend crucial All-Ireland Hurling Final.

95 mph. Bertie Ahern 2002

Journalists 'clock' canvassing Taoiseach at 95mph. Ahern rejects slur. Blames "travelling press" for delaying re-election convoy.

95 mph. Noel Treacy 2003

Treacy's emergency dash prompted by highest calling — to speak in Dáil. Cites solemn duty "to be available" to serve Ireland.

OPENING LINES OF IRISH BOOKS

Theresa had told me on the phone that I was Disgraced World Cup Star Roy Keane. *Keane: The Autobiography.*

The studio was filled with the rich odour of roses, and when the light summer wind stirred amidst the trees of the garden, there came through the open door the heavy scent of the lilac, or the more delicate perfume of the pink-flowering thorn. *The Picture of Dorian Gray, Oscar Wilde.*

Not everybody knows how I killed old Phillip Mathers, smashing his jaws in with my spade; but first it is better to speak of my friendship with John Divney because it was he who first knocked old Mathers down by giving him a great blow in the neck with a special bicycle pump which he manufactured himself out of a hollow iron bar. *The Third Policeman, Flann O'Brien.*

When I was a young lad twenty or thirty or forty years ago, I lived in a small town where they were all after me on account of what I done on Mrs Nugent. *The Butcher Boy, Patrick McCabe.*

I was four, or perhaps just five, playing on the study floor, my mother seated near me. I made a derogatory remark about the Protestant religion of the then Vice-President of the Executive Council, Ernest Blythe. *All in a Life, Garret Fitzgerald.*

PUT THAT IN YOUR PIPE

The word didgeridoo comes from the Irish language, says academic Dymphna Lonergan. She believes Irish settlers in Australia called it a 'dudaire duth'. 'Dudaire' means 'pipe-smoker' or 'horn-blower' while 'duth', pronounced 'doo', means 'native'. The Irish word 'dubh' (black) is an alternative root of 'doo'. 'Didgeridoo' has nothing in common with the aboriginal language. Lonergan also discovered an Irish origin for the term 'warm the cockles of your heart'. The old Irish word 'cohaill' literally means 'the membrane of the heart'.

NURSE, THE SCREENS!

FOUR ARGUMENTS TO GOVT FOR AN IRISH TV SERVICE, 1953

1. Ireland needs TV service to counter cultural pollution of UK 'overspill' signals.
2. TV could promote work of the Church and spread message of Christ to troubled souls.
3. With the support of the (wary) State, the service could be on air within one year.
4. For national coverage, signals could bounce off an aircraft continually circling midlands.

Proposed by 'television enthusiast' Eric Boden on Radio Éireann, Feb 1953.

SHOW SOME CONCERN, 1985

Celebrity 45 for Ethiopia, performed by 'The Concerned':

Christy Moore
Red Hurley
Maxi & Twink
Flo McSweeney
Linda Martin
Ray Lynam

Members of:
Auto Da Fe
The Blades
Blue in Heaven
Clannad
Fastaway
The Host
Light a Big Fire
Stockton's Wing
Toy with Rhythm
Those Nervous Animals

THE TWELVE IRISH-AMERICAN MAYORS OF BOSTON

1885-88: Hugh O'Brien. Born Fermanagh. Businessman. Low tax, anti-corruption.

1902-05: Patrick Collins. Born Cork. Same policies. Half of Boston population now Irish.

1905: Daniel Whelton. Four-month term. Jobs for the boys. Irish influence strengthened.

*1906-13:** John Fitzgerald. JFK's grandfather, Wexford parents. Confrontational style.

*1914-49:** James Curley. Slogan: "vote early and often". Jailed for fraud as Mayor. Pardoned.

1934-37: Frederick Mansfield. Low-spending lawyer. Known as 'Ferocious Freddie'.

1938-44: Maurice Tobin. Later Gov of Mass and US Sec for Labour. Consensus seeker.

1945: John Kerrigan. Quiet. Mayor after Tobin elected as State Gov. Beaten by Curley.

1950-59: John Hynes. Quiet, anti-corruption. Acting Mayor in 1947 when Curley was jailed.

1960-67: John Collins. Lawyer. Reshaped 'New Boston'. City Hall Plaza named after him.

1968-83: Kevin White. First 4-in-a-row Mayor. Promoted city to outsiders. Consensus man.

1984-93: Raymond Flynn. 3 terms. Urban renewal. Later US Ambassador to Vatican.

* Fitzgerald 1906–07, 1910–13; Curley 1914–17, 1922–25, 1930–33, 1946–49 (after pardon, lost to Hynes in 1949). All members of Democratic Party.

TALES FROM THE MONTROSE CRYPT

1970s: Maggie Riordan's Phantom Pregnancy
Unwed Maggie clearly expecting. Writer told make her ill instead.

1978: 'The Spike' is Spiked Mid-Series
Brief nudity Episode 5. Episode 6 ditched for priest documentary.

1992: 'Scrap Saturday' is Not Scrapped
Irish radio's lone must-hear show is merely "not continued".

1993: Making a Drama out of a Comedy
TV comedy 'Extra Extra' makes debut. Introduced as "new drama".

IRISH GIRL GUIDES' TOOTHBRUSH SONG

Tune: Oh My Darling Clementine

Little Mary had a toothbrush, and she hung it on the wall.
Did she use it? Did she use it? Did she use it? Not at all.

Then one morning, at the table, she began to scream and shout:
"Oh! my Mommy, I've a toothache! Will I have to get it out?"

Then Mommy took her to the dentist,
and the dentist shook his head:
"It's too late for little Mary.
She should have brushed her teeth instead."

WHAT DO IRISH COUNTY & CITY NAMES MEAN?

Antrim	The Solitary Farm	Laois	* The Laoigis
Armagh	Macha's Height	Leitrim	Grey Hill-Ridge
Belfast	Ford of the Sandbank	Limerick	River of Cloaks
Carlow	Quadruple Lake	Longford	O'Farrell's Fort
Cavan	The Hollow	Louth	The River Lud
Clare	The Plain	Mayo	Plain of Ewe Trees
Cork	The Marsh	Meath	The Middle
Derry	The Oak Grove	Monaghan	Place of Shrubs
Donegal	Foreigners' Fort	Offaly	Failghe's People
Down	The Fort	Rathdown	An old Irish Barony
Dublin	Black Pool	Roscommon	Coman's Height
Dun Laoghaire	Laoghaire's Fort	Sligo	Abounding in Shells
Fermanagh	Manach's Men	Tipperary	The Well of Ara
Fingal	White Foreigner	Tyrone	Eoghan's Territory
Galway	Galvia's River	Waterford	Weather Haven
Kerry	Ciar's People	Westmeath	West Central
Kildare	Oak Tree Church	Wexford	Fjord of the Flats
Kilkenny	Cainneach's Church	Wicklow	Viking Meadow

* The Laoigis were a tribe of Iron-age Picts.

IRISH CONDOMS AFTER "THE IRISH SOLUTION"

1980: After Haughey's "Irish solution to an Irish problem" Health Act, 9m condoms are imported in three months.

1985: Garret Fitzgerald's Govt amends the law: anyone over 18 can buy a condom without a prescription. Fianna Fáil expels Des O'Malley after his "I stand by the Republic" support of condoms. FF's Pee Flynn tells Dáil: "The fashionable length of a lady's skirt or the width of a gent's trousers might change but the right for young unmarried teenagers to fornicate is still unnatural and wrong."

1986: Leitrim FF Cllr Joseph Mary Mooney (Paschal's dad) wants Health Minister Barry Desmond to be prosecuted under the Explosives Act for legalising condoms.

1991: Irish Family Planning Association fined for selling condoms in Virgin Megastore. Richard Branson lends support.

1992: Amid fear of AIDS (and despite the campaign booklet *67 Reasons Why Condoms Spread AIDS*), age of purchase is reduced to 17. Shops and pubs can now sell them, but only over the counter.

1996: Euro Commissioner Pee Flynn distributes 300,000 condoms throughout Europe in St Valentine's Day cards. Green MEP Patricia McKenna hopes that Pee "will continue to promote condoms from Copenhagen to Castlebar".

In 2003 the average Irish family has 1.6 children (it had eight in 1911).

ARTHUR MURPHY'S MAILBOX

THREE MEMORABLE MISSIVES

Complaint that tractor in farm show was driven incompetently.

Complaint that forks of TV fork-lift truck were at wrong height.

Home-video from regular Welsh correspondent in all-male orgy.

(Highest number of gripes to mailbox came from Cork)

THE HEROIC OFFERING

THE PRAYER OF THE PIONEER TOTAL ABSTINENCE ASSOCIATION

For Thy greater glory and consolation, O Sacred Heart of Jesus,
for Thy sake to give good example,
to practise self-denial, to make reparation
to Thee for the sins of intemperance,
and for the conversion of excessive drinkers,
I will abstain for life from all intoxicating drinks. Amen.

The rules of being a Pioneer: Keep the pledge. Wear the pin. Recite the prayer twice daily.

Optional: Matt Talbot wore a chain around his body to remind himself of his Pioneer pledge.

SPOT THE DIFFERENCE

FF Website Nov 2000	*FF Website June 2003*
Bertie Ahern, Education:	*Bertie Ahern, Education:*
St Patrick's NS, Drumcondra	St Patrick's NS, Drumcondra
St Aidan's CBS, Whitehall	St Aidan's CBS, Whitehall
College of Commerce, Rathmines	College of Commerce, Rathmines
University College Dublin	University College Dublin
London School of Economics	

When reporters could not trace Ahern's UCD or LSE attendance records, his spokesperson said: "He has never claimed to hold degrees from UCD or anywhere else… he remembers doing the courses, but not what they were."

THE COMMITMENTS

Creator	Roddy Doyle	*Trumpet*	'The Lips' Fagan
Manager	Jimmy Rabbitte	*Piano*	Steve Clifford
Singer	Deco Cuffe	*Drummer*	Mikah Wallace
Guitar	Outspan Foster	*Singer*	Imelda Quirke
Bass	Derek Scully	*Singer*	Bernie McGloughlin
Saxophone	Dean Fay	*Singer*	Natalie Murphy

FAN MAIL SENT TO SHEEBA

"Do you remember me? I was the one in the front wearing the black anorak. I chatted to you after the show and you said you'd meet me out front but you never did."

"Would you come down if I sent you the train fare?"

"I've been a great fan of yours for many years, though not of your singing. I read somewhere that you like tall, skinny men. I'm a tall, skinny man."

"I've got a big farm. I'd like to marry the one in the middle. Are you interested?"

(1+3 to Maxi, 2 to Twink, 4 to all after a TV appearance.)

PAT KENNY AND THE LADY IN RED

Chris de Burgh's 'Lady In Red' was No 1 in 25 countries and sold over 8 million copies. De Burgh wrote the line "never seen so many men ask you if you wanted to dance" after he saw his wife Diane dancing in a Stillorgan nightclub with RTE's 'Late Late Show' presenter Pat Kenny.

ONLY LITTLE PEOPLE PAY TAX

1988: Finance Minister Albert Reynolds announces a "once off" tax amnesty.

1993: Reynolds as Taoiseach gives tax cheats one last ever chance to come clean.

1993: Attorney General advises that amnesty looks unconstitutional. Reynolds presses ahead regardless.

1993: Finance Minister Bertie Ahern warns of amnesty's "serious negative impact".

1993: Amnesty comes to cabinet. Ahern proposes it.

2001: Bogus account holders, liable for jail or fines for breaking their 1993 promises, get comeuppance with final, final amnesty.

FANTASY FOOTBALL MATCH

IRISH FOOTBALL INTERNATIONALS WHO PLAYED MOST OF THEIR CAREERS IN THE LEAGUE OF IRELAND

60-80s: Mick
1. Smyth

70-80s: Eamon *2. Gregg* | 80-90s: Barry *4. Murphy* | 50-70s: Johnny *5. Fullam* | 70-80s: Pat *3. Byrne*

60-70s: Frank *6. O'Neill* | 50-60s: Ronnie *8. Nolan* | 50-60s: Liam *10. Tuohy*

50-70s: Paddy *7. Ambrose* | 60-80s: Turly *9. O'Connor* | 60-70s: Mick *11. Leech*

60-70s: Tony *22. O'Connell* | 70-80s: Mick *20. Fairclough* | 70-80s: Cathal *18. Muckian*

70-90s: Synan *21. Braddish* | 60-80s: Mick *19. Lawlor* | 30-50s: Jackie *17. O'Reilly*

60-70s: John *14. Herrick* | 60-70s: Al *16. Finucane* | 60-80s: Tommy *15. McConville* | 40-50s: Florrie *13. Burke*

60-80s: Peter
12. Thomas

Athlone: 1, 4, 5, 9, 21. Bohemians: 1, 2, 3, 4, 5, 8, 9, 11, 22. Cobh: 3. Cork Hibs: 14. Cork Utd/Ath: 13, 17. Drumcondra: 1. Drogheda: 18, 20. Dundalk: 2, 9, 15, 18, 19, 20, 21, 22. Home Farm: 6, 19. Kilkenny: 2, 4, 21. Limerick: 14, 16. Longford: 21. St Pats: 2, 4, 11, 21. Shelbourne: 3, 18, 19. Shamrock Rovers: 1, 2, 3, 4, 5, 6, 7, 8, 10, 11, 18, 19, 22. Sligo Rovers: 20. Waterford: 6, 11, 12, 15, 16.

And still playing: Glen Crowe (Bohemians), first capped 2002.

NORTHERN IRISH ANAGRAMS

PROTESTANT PARLIAMENT	ALERT! RAMPANT NEPOTIST
GERRY ADAMS	*A DREGS ARMY*
GOOD FRIDAY AGREEMENT	A FINE MERRY DOG-EAT-DOG

TOP ANCESTRIES IN USA

Ancestry	*Millions*	*of Pop*	*Ancestry*	*Millions*	*of Pop*
German	42.9	15.2 %	Italian	15.7	5.6 %
Irish	30.5	10.8 %	Polish	8.9	3.2 %
English	24.5	8.7 %	French	8.3	3.0 %
United States	20.6	7.3 %	Scottish	4.9	1.7 %

Census 2000. Includes single and multiple ancestries.

MEN OF FEW WORDS

LEAST SAID IN THE 37TH DÁIL, 1997-2002

TD	*Party*	*Spoke For*	*2002 Election*
Liam Burke	FG	1 min 30 secs	Didn't stand
Tom Gildea	Ind	7 min 40 secs	Didn't stand
Albert Reynolds	FF	15 minutes	Didn't stand

Tom Gildea accused ex-Justice Min Nora Owen of abusing the Gardaí, refused to withdraw the allegation, caused the House to be suspended, withdrew the allegation, asked on a point of order for another minute and half of speaking time, then apologised the next day. Quietest to be re-elected were Michael Lowry 38 mins and Jackie Healy-Rae 39 mins.

MOST POPULAR IRISH CARS

BASED ON PRIVATE CARS LICENSED IN MARCH 2003

New	*Cars*	*%*	*Second-hand*	*Cars*	*%*
Ford	2,004	10.8	Toyota	121	11.9
Volkswagon	1,913	10.3	Ford	96	9.5
Toyota	1,895	10.2	Volkswagon	80	7.9
Opel	1,801	9.7	Mercedes-Benz	74	7.3
Nissan	1,619	8.7	Nissan	72	7.1

CSO 2003. There were 18,567 new private cars licensed in March 2003, compared to 21,391 in March 2002 and 22,146 in March 2001.

I WAS MORTO!

SIX 'MOST EMBARRASSING MOMENTS'

Ann Doyle "My knickers falling down in Woolworths."	*Bob Geldof* Introducing Tanzanian leader Nyerere. Wrong man.
Terry Keane "My knickers falling down in Baggots of Baggot Street."	*Paddy Prendeville* Caught by Brian Lenihan Snr rifling Lenihan's office files.
Sen Shane Ross Meeting Gay Byrne and asking what he did for a living.	*Mary Coughlan* Failing to win talent contest. Smashing 1st prize trophy.

Prendeville Editor of *Phoenix;* Coughlan singer not Minister.

OLD IRISH TERRITORIAL UNITS

Approximate Division		*Equals*		*Approx Acres*
10	Acres	= 1	Gneeve	10
2	Gneeves	= 1	Sessiagh	20
3	Sessiagh	= 1	Tate	60
2	Tates or Ballyboes	= 1	Ploughland	120
4	Ploughlands, Seisreagh or Carrows	= 1	Townland	480
?	Townlands or Ballybetaghs	= 1	Barony	Varied

Names of, and relationships between, divisions varied around the country.

TWO CUTE FOCAILS

Jim Tunney, as chair of the FF parliamentary party, saved CJ Haughey from a no confidence vote in 1983. Speaking in Irish, he adjourned the meeting and quickly left before TDs realised that he had given CJ a weekend to 'convince' waverers.

Prionsias De Rossa, as Social Welfare Minister, was accused of misleading the Dáil about appointing advisers in 1996. He apologised during private members' time, speaking Irish, forgiving Michael McDowell and others for insulting him.

PAPAL YOUTH MASS, GALWAY, 1979

REPRESENTATIVES TO BE SENT FROM EACH DIOCESE FOR THE OFFERTORY PROCESSION

1. A National School Teacher with a Cap and Gown	6. A Carpenter's Apprentice in Dungarees
2. A Married Couple and Baby	7. A Baker in White Overalls
3. A Blind Person	8. A Farmer and a Dog
4. An Athlete	9. An Irish Dancer
5. A Lame Person with a Stick or Crutches	10. An Itinerant
	11. A Deaf Person

JOYCE'S ODYSSEY

THE DUBLIN HOMES OF JAMES JOYCE

Born in 1882 in *41 Brighton Square,* Rathgar; moved age 2 to *23 Castlewood Ave,* Rathmines; moved age 5 to *1 Martello Tce,* Bray; when age 6, attended Clongowes Wood boarding school, Sallins, Kildare; moved age 9 to *Leoville, 23 Carysfort Ave,* Blackrock; moved age 10 to *29 Hardwicke St,* now demolished, and *14 FitzGibbon St,* now number 34;	moved age 12 to *2 Millbourne Ave,* Drumcondra, now demolished; moved age 13 to *17 Nth Richmond St;* moved age 17 to *29 Windsor Ave, 7 Convent Ave* and *13 Richmond Ave,* all Fairview; moved age 18 to *8 Royal Tce,* Fairview, now Inverness Road; moved age 19 to *32 Glengariff Pde,* Nth Circular Rd; moved age 20 to *8 St Peter's Tce,* Phibsboro; moved age 20	to Paris; returned at 21 when mother was dying; moved at 22 to *60 Shelbourne Rd,* Ballsbridge, *39 Strand Rd,* Sandymount, *103 Nth Strand Rd,* Fairview and *Martello Tower,* Sandycove; left Ireland with Nora Barnacle age 22; returned briefly age 25 and 26 to *44 Fontenoy St* visiting *Bloom Hse at 7 Eccles Street;* and age 30 to *17-21 Richmond Pl,* now 609 and 617 Nth Circular Rd.

THE 'BETTER HEALTH CUTS' OF 1987

Pre-Election: FF billboards predict: "Health cuts hurt the old, the sick and the handicapped: there is a better way."

Post-Election: "Brace yourself, Bridget!" says FF spin-master PJ Mara, announcing the Govt's new and better health cuts.

Later: Forgetful Taoiseach Charles Haughey says he "was not personally aware" of the hardship caused. Health Min Rory O'Hanlon insists waiting lists "are a very unreliable measure of the availability of hospital services".

THE FIVE BEST IRELAND FOOTBALL MANAGERS, EVER!

Manager	*Years*	*P*	*W*	*D*	*Pts*	*%*
Alan Kelly	1980	1	1	0	3	100
Jack Charlton	1986-96	94	47	30	171	61
Mick McCarthy	1996-03	68	29	20	107	52
Johnny Giles	1973-80	37	14	9	51	46
Eoin Hand	1980-86	40	11	9	42	35

Calculated at 3 points for a win. Alan Kelly's 100% record is a 2-0 win against Switzerland in April 1980, with Don Givens and Gerry Daly scoring. Brian Kerr's record for his first 10 games was 6 wins, 3 draws, 21 pts, 70%.

CAN'T SING, LOOK AWFUL

1976: Jim Hand Turns Down the Boomtown Rats
Showband impresario says he rejected the band as "brutal".

1979: CBS Records International Turn Down U2
CBS Ireland had signed fab four. London HQ unimpressed.

1979: Riva Records' Talent Scout Makes U2 Gaffe
Billy Gaff comes to see U2. Gets drunk. Signs The Lookalikes.

*1998: Louis Walsh Passes Up B*Witched*
Group with 2 sisters of Boyzone's Keith Duffy sell millions.

NOT JUST A PRETTY FACE

FIVE FAMOUS SPOTS OF AMATEUR DRAMATICS

1970s: Albert Reynolds Proud to be in Cowboy Outfit
P&T Min sings "put your sweet lips closer to phone".

1988: Minister Burke Upstages Winner at Eurovision
Rambo belts out 'Molly Malone'. Celine Dion belts-up.

1992: Peter Brooke Hits a Bum Note on 'Late Late'
NI Secretary sings on TV on day IRA bomb kills 8.

1996: Denis O'Brien Makes Lead Balloon Joke
Jogging Esat boss jokes he passed £200K to Lowry and others.

2003: Enda Kenny Prepares for the Presidency
Fine Gael leader does JFK impression on Dunphy Show.

WHAT 'FOOT & MOUTH' COST IRELAND

Gains to Agricultural Sector		*Losses Elsewhere*	
Pig sector	€ 9 million	Tourist sector	€ 210 million
Sheep sector	€ 23 million	Dept of Agriculture	€ 44 million
Beef sector	€ 30 million	Gardaí	€ 50 million
Multiplier effect	€ 44 million	Promoting tourism	€13 million
Total	€ 106 million	Total	€ 317 million

Dept Agriculture 2002. Farmers got firmer prices and greater exports to UK.

MR VERSATILITY

Kevin O'Flanagan played both football and rugby for Ireland, scoring on his football debut in 1937. He was also a four-time Irish long-jump champ from 1938-43, Irish sprint champ in 1941 and captained Bohemians to an Irish Cup win in 1945.

He then moved to England (to work as a doctor) where he played football for Arsenal and rugby for London Irish. In his spare time he played tennis and single-stroke-handicap golf. He later became team doctor to the Irish Olympic squad.

TWO UNUSUAL IRISH DEATHS

Johannes Scotus Eriugena was the monk and philosopher on the old £5 note. In 877 his students reputedly stabbed him to death with pens for trying to make them think too hard.

Sir Arthur Aston led Drogheda resistance against Cromwell in 1649. Enemy soldiers beat him to death with his own wooden leg. They mistakenly believed it to contain gold.

FIVE GREAT IRISH ECCENTRICS

Benjamin O'Neill Stratford. Baltinglass, Wicklow. Aim: To secretly build world's biggest balloon in giant barn. Outcome: After 20 years, barn and balloon destroyed by fire. Reaction: Retreated to Spanish hotel, living on room service. When suite was full of dirty crockery he'd change rooms.

Mary Monckton, Lady Cork. Distinction: Lavish dinners attracted Johnson, Byron, etc. 'Tendency': Stole compulsively and randomly. One of her maid's duties was to sift booty and return to rightful owners. Impulses: Stole a pet hedgehog which turned cranky. Swapped it for a sponge cake.

Richard Whately. C of I Dublin Archbishop 1831-1863. Distinction: Uncontrollable legs. Hyperactive. Involuntary wrecker of furniture. Celebrity status: His sermons became a popular spectator sport. Hobbies: Boomerang throwing, tree-climbing, gardening in clerical robes.

Robert 'Linen' Cook. Farmer, Cappaquin, County Waterford. Obsession: White. Wore only white linen. Barred black cattle and horses from his land. Disposition: 16th Century vegan. Caught fox attacking his poultry. Lectured fox on 5th Commandment (Thou Shalt Not Kill) and released fox.

The Third, 'Mad', Marquis of Waterford. 'Mad'?: Squandered fortune on pranks. Donated gin to London's poor. Drunken riots ensued. Marquis arrested. Horse-sense: Arrested for speeding on horse in built-up area. Rode horse into court as witness. Claimed horse alone knew its speed. Acquitted.

INDEX OF TOPICS